The seventh edition of the
Best of European Design and Advertising from the Art Directors Club of Europe 1998

THE ART DIRECTORS CLUB OF EUROPE WAS FOUNDED IN JUNE 1990 AS A NOT-FOR-PROFIT ORGANIS-ATION TO FOSTER AND REWARD CREATIVE EXCELLENCE IN EUROPEAN DESIGN AND ADVERTISING. → IT IS MANAGED AND OWNED BY THE 12 REPRESENTATIVE NATIONAL BODIES ACROSS EUROPE. EACH OF THESE ORGANISATIONS HAS A MEMBERSHIP OF LEADING PROFESSIONAL CREATIVES AND EACH ONE ALSO RUNS ITS COUNTRY'S PREMIER AWARDS SCHEME. → ONLY THE TOP AWARDS FROM EACH NATIONAL COMPETITION ARE ELIGIBLE FOR ENTRY TO THE ART DIRECTORS CLUB OF EUROPE. ALL OF THESE PIECES ARE FEATURED IN THE ANNUAL PROVIDING A UNIQUE EUROPEAN ARCHIVE. → FOUR SENIOR CREATIVES PER COUNTRY ARE SENT TO JUDGE THIS BODY OF WORK MAKING A TOTAL JURY OF UP TO 50 LEADING ART DIRECTORS, COPYWRITERS, DESIGNERS, PHOTOGRAPHERS AND COMMERCIALS DIRECTORS. THEY SELECT GOLD AWARDS IN EACH CATEGORY AND AN OVERALL GRAND PRIX. → THE BOOK IS DISTRIBUTED TO ALL THE 8,000 MEMBERS OF ALL THE INDIVIDUAL NATIONAL CLUBS AND IS ALSO SOLD IN BOOKSHOPS AROUND THE WORLD.

THREE YEARS AGO I ATTENDED MY FIRST ADCE BOARD MEETING. SINCE THAT MEETING THERE HAS BEEN TWO MAJOR CHANGES. THE FIRST, RATHER BORINGLY BUT IMPORTANTLY, IS HOW THE ADCE IS FINANCED. IT IS NOW FUNDED BY THE MEMBER CLUBS ON A SLIDING SCALE OF THEIR INCOME, A LITTLE LESS VOLATILE THAN RELYING SOLELY ON ENTRY NUMBERS. → THE OTHER IMPORTANT CHANGE IS HOW THE WORK IS JUDGED. ONLY WORK THAT HAS WON A SILVER OR GOLD IN ITS OWN COUNTRY'S AWARD SCHEME IS ELIGIBLE FOR ENTRY TO THE ADCE AWARDS. THIS DISTINGUISHES THE ADCE FROM EVERY OTHER AWARD SCHEME AND TRULY POSITIONS THE WINNING WORK AS THE BEST IN EUROPE. → WHAT A RELIEF THAT IN MY THIRD YEAR, AS PRESIDENT, THE INTEGRITY OF THOSE DECISIONS IS EVIDENT IN THIS BOOK. → ALMOST WITHOUT EXCEPTION. I BELIEVE THE WINNING WORK THIS YEAR WOULD GRACE THE WALLS AND REELS OF ANY AGENCY IN EUROPE. IF YOU TAKE A LITTLE MORE TIME YOU'LL FIND THE ODD GEM IN THIS ANNUAL THAT DIDN'T QUITE MAKE IT. → A FEW MORE CHANGES THIS YEAR; FIRSTLY, THE NETHERLANDS HAVE JOINED. GIVEN THE CONSISTENT QUALITY OF THEIR WORK I AM SURE THEIR PRESENCE IS GOING TO BE FELT QUITE DRAMATICALLY AND QUICKLY. → ALSO THE SECRETARIAT HAS THIS YEAR MOVED TO D&AD'S OFFICES IN LONDON. THIS NEATLY BRINGS ME TO A FEW ACKNOWLEDGEMENTS. A SPECIAL THANKS TO DAVID KESTER FOR HIS UNBENDING SUPPORT AND TIRELESS ENERGY AND TO LOUISA NEALE AT D&AD WHO NOW ALMOST RUNS THE WHOLE THING. TO OUR SPONSORS FOR TAKING ADVERTISING SPACE, BEN CASEY AT THE CHASE FOR COUNTLESS FAVOURS AND LASTLY TO EVERYONE WHO OVER THE LAST THREE YEARS HAS CONTRIBUTED TIME AND AN IDEA. → **PETER GATLEY**, PRESIDENT.

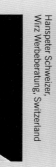

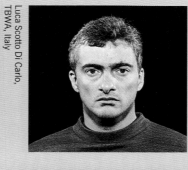

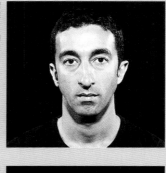 

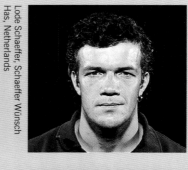

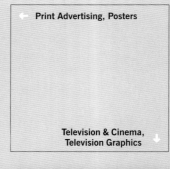

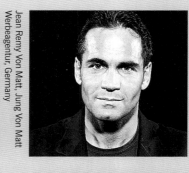 

Chairman: David Croft, Ireland

Alexander Kellas, Demner, Merlicek & Bergmann, Austria

Jean Werner, TBWA, Belgium

Sebastian Turner, Scholz & Friends, Germany

Mike Garner, Ogilvy One Worldwide, Ireland

Enzo Baldoni, La Balena Colpiscono Ancora, Italy

Aad Kuijper, Lowe Kuijper & Schouter, Netherlands

Aris Theophilakis, Bates Backer, Norway

Anna Nyström, Allansson & Nilsson, Sweden

Hanspeter Schweizer, Wirz Werbeberatung, Switzerland

John Messum, HHCL & Partners, UK

← Print Advertising, Posters

Television & Cinema, Television Graphics ↓

Chairman: Luigi Montaini Anelli, Italy

Anthony F Guedes, Film Factory, Austria

Philippe Thito, DDB, Belgium

Jean Remy Von Matt, Jung Von Matt, Werbeagentur, Germany

Laurence Keogh, Dimension Advertising, Ireland

Luca Scotto Di Carlo, TBWA, Italy

Lode Schaeffer, Schaeffer Wünsch Has, Netherlands

Thorbjørn Naug, Bates Backer, Norway

Manuel de Luque, Anuncios, Spain

Frank Hollingworth, Hollingworth/Mehrotra, Sweden

Martin Fueter, Condor Films, Switzerland

Richard Flintham, BMP.DDB, UK

Chairman: Martin Spillmann, Switzerland

Lo Breier, Buro X (Hamburg), Austria

Werner Van Reck, LDV & Partners, Belgium

Kurt Georg Dieckert, Springer & Jacoby, Germany

Robin Hegarty, Language, Ireland

Gabriella Ambrosio, Ambrosio Maoloni, Italy

Anton Beeke, Studio Anton Beeke, Netherlands

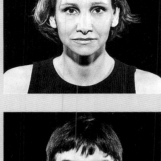

Kristine Lillevik, Scandinavian Design Group, Norway

Fernando Gutiérrez, Grafica, Spain

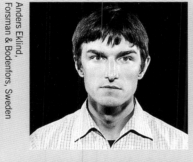

Anders Eklind, Forsman & Bodenfors, Sweden

Iréne Hiltbold, Freelance, Switzerland

Shaun Dew, Dew Gibbons, UK

Graphic Design, Packaging & Promotion

Chairman: Marco Calant, Belgium

Christoffr Steinegger, Haslinger Keck Advertising, Austria

Gino Del Ben, Grey, Belgium

Editorial, Illustration & Photography →

Federica Ariagno, Saatchi & Saatchi, Italy

Hans Wolf, VNU Tijdschriftengroep bv, Netherlands

Svein Størksen, Freelance, Norway

Björn Kusoffsky, Kusoffsky, Sweden

Simone Fennel, Freelance, Switzerland

Jim Sutherland, HGV Design, UK

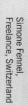

Art Directors Club Europe
9 Graphite Square
Vauxhall Walk
London
SE11 5EE
Co-ordinator: Louisa Neale
T: 00 44 171 840 1113
F: 00 44 171 840 0840

Administration

Members of ADCE

Austria
Creativ Club Austria
Kochgasse 34/16
A-1080 Wien

Belgium
Creative Club of Belgium
4 rue Jean d'Ardenne
B-1050 Brussels

Denmark
Creative Circle Denmark
Nyhavn 12b
1051 København K

Germany
Art Directors Club für Deutschland
Melemstrasse 22
60322 Frankfurt

Ireland
Institute of Creative Advertising and Design
31 Heytesbury Lane
Dublin 4

Italy
Art Directors Club Italiano
Via Sant'Orsola 1
20123 Italy

The Netherlands
ADCN
W G Plein 504
1054 SJ Amsterdam

Norway
Kreativt Forum
PO Box 2660 Solli
0203 Oslo

Spain
ADG.FAD
Brusi 45
08006 Barcelona

Sweden
Sveriges Reklamförbund
Norrlandsgatan 24
Box 1420
111 84 Stockholm

Switzerland
Art Directors Club Schweiz
Oberdorfstrasse 15
8001 Zürich

UK
British Design and Art Direction
9 Graphite Square
Vauxhall Walk
London
SE11 5EE

Board of Directors

President
Peter Gatley, UK

Treasurer
Johannes Newrkla, Austria

Controller
David Kester, UK

Johannes Newrkla, Austria
Marco Calant, Belgium
Ib Borup, Denmark
Othmar Severin, Germany
David Croft, Ireland
Luigi Montaini Anelli, Italy
Krijn Van Noordwijk, The Netherlands
Fred Hauge, Norway
Fernando Gutiérrez, Spain
Christer Allansson, Sweden
Martin Spillmann, Switzerland

Art Directors
Club of Europe 1998
Contents

Grand Prix
TV & Cinema Advertising
Television Commercial

National Award UK Silver
Title The Lamp Post, Hiccups, Chair, Dentist.
Agency BMP DDB
Client Volkswagen Group
Creative Director Jeremy Craigen
Art Director Andrew Fraser
Copywriter Andrew Fraser
Agency Producer Howard Spivey
Production Company Outsider

Lamp Post
We see two men at work in a residential street. One is wrapping padding around a lamp post, and the other is putting up a poster. When the men have finished, they drive off in their van. As the van pulls away, we see that the poster says, 'Polo, only £8,145'.
After they have gone, a man in a suit walks into frame, and turns to look at the poster. He carries on walking and staring at the poster, unaware that he is about to bump into the lamp post. We now realise what the padding is for.

Hiccups
A woman is sitting at her kitchen table reading a newspaper. She is suffering from hiccups. Finally, she comes across an ad in the paper which says 'Polo, from only £7,990'. The hiccups are cured.

Chair
A woman is walking through a shopping precinct. Suddenly she feels faint, and starts to lose her balance. A passer-by comes over and helps her to a nearby bench. When, eventually, she starts to recover, she looks back along the precinct, and we see what caused the problem. There is a poster, which says 'Polo, from only £7,990'.

Dentist
A dentist tries, unsuccessfully, to persuade a patient to open his mouth wider. Finally, he tells the patient that he's just bought a Golf Gti for only £14,640. The patient's mouth drops open for him.

Surprisingly ordinary prices.

www.volkswagen.co.uk

Surprisingly ordinary prices.

www.volkswagen.co.uk

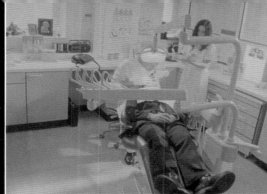

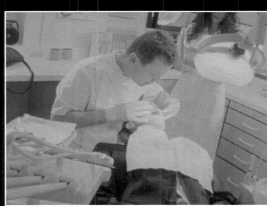

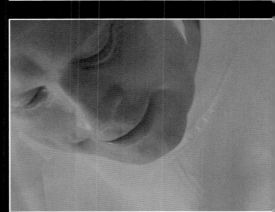

Polo,
from only
£7,990.

Polo L

Surprisingly ordinary prices.

www.volkswagen.co.uk

Surprisingly ordinary prices.

www.volkswagen.co.uk

1 **Nomination**
   Editorial

   National Award Gold
   Title Five
   Design Studio Haslinger, Keck
   Client Sabotage Communications
   Creative Directors Christoph Steinegger
   Robert Jelinek
   Art Director Christoph Steinegger
   Copywriters Justin Hoffmann
   Robert Jelinek
   Designer Christoph Steinegger
   Photographers Udo Titz
   Slava Fillippow

2 **Nomination**
   Illustration & Photography
   Photography

   National Award Silver
   Title Reprozwölf
   Design Studio Bárci & Partner
   Client Reprozwölf
   Creative Director Marco De Felice
   Art Director Marco De Felice
   Photographer Elfie Semotan

   Reproduction down to the essentials.

hide & seek

3

3 Nomination
Illustration & Photography
Photography

National Award Gold
Title Hide and seek
Agency Haslinger, Keck
Client D & C
Creative Directors Christoph
Steinegger Udo Titz
Art Director Christoph Steinegger
Copywriter Norbert Tomasi
Designers E Feichtl M Reiter
Ch Schöffler M Schinwald
Photographer Udo Titz

4 Print Advertising
Newspaper Advertising

National Award Silver
Title Mazda 323 2.0l
Agency Demner, Merlicek &
Bergmann
Client Mazda Austria
Creative Directors Johannes Newrkla
Stephan Klein Daniel Mayer
Art Director Mag. Francesco Bestagno
Copywriters Stephan Klein
Helge Haberzettl
Photographer Staudinger Franke
Illustrator Hannes Glantschnig

Teaser: Austria's most sold car is about
to show you a new side.
Solution: Austria's most sold car with a
different touch: The new 2.0 fuel
injected diesel in the Mazda 323.

Gleich zeigt Ihnen
Österreichs meistverkaufter Benziner
eine ganz neue Seite.

Der neue 2,0 l Einspritz-Diesel
im Mazda 323.

4

1. Siemens: Reading comes before
image.
2. max mobil: What would a mobile
phone be without reading?
3. profile: Reading comes before
culture.

5

6

1

2

3

1

2

3

4

7 Print Advertising
Magazine Advertising

National Award Silver
Title Concerto Abo-campaign
Agency Projektgruppe "Arsch & Freidrich"
Client Concerto Magazine
Art Directors Peter Burgstaller
Hubert Goldnagl
Creative Directors Walter Robisch
Andreas Schalko
Photographers Hubert Goldnagl
Peter Burgstaller
Illustrator Ander Pecher
Copywriters Walter Robisch
Andreas Schalko

1. The first abo-ad with an ect-foto.
2. Speech for Christmas, very rough draft, top secret! Dear Austrian women and men...
3. The Concerto European Tour 97.
4. You miserable chauvanistic pig!

★
8

8 TV & Cinema Advertising
Television Commercial

National Award Silver
Title Kodak
Agency Lowe GGK Wien
Client Kodak Fotoservice
Creative Director Chrigel Ott
Art Director Daniel Gantner
Copywriter Michael Dobesch
Agency Producer Ulli Wendl
Production Company
PPM Filmproductions
Director of Photography
Josh Josimovic
Film Director Josh Josimovic

The best pictures - that's for sure - are original from Kodak - or nothing!

9 **TV & Cinema Advertising**
Cinema Commercial

National Award Silver
Title What's news?
Agency Demner, Merlicek & Bergmann
Client News
Art Director Tomek Luczynski
Copywriter Mag Gerda Schebesta
Film Director Louis Pascal Couvelaire
Director of Photography Michel Abramovicz
Production Company Adi Meyer Film
Agency Producer Waltraud Broż

10 **TV & Cinema Advertising**
Cinema Commercial

National Award Gold
Title Birthday Zürich
Agency Demner, Merlicek & Bergmann
Client Media Markt Switzerland
Art Director Elisabeth Sauter
Creative Director Dr. Angelo Peer
Copywriter Cosima Reif
Agency Producer Waltraud Broż
Film Director Paul Harather
Director of Photography Andreas Hutter
Production Company Adi Mayer Film

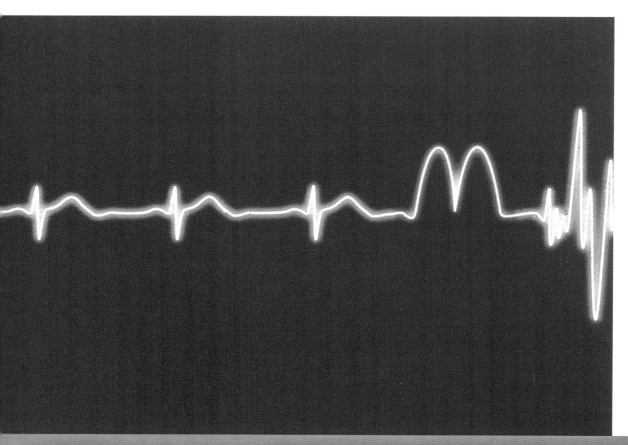

11 **TV & Cinema Advertising**
Television Commercial

National Award Gold
Title Gone to the dogs
Agency Dachverband Der
österreichischen Filmsch Affenden
Client Dachverband Der
österreichischen Filmsch Affenden (DLF)
Creative Director
Dr. Maria Anna Kollmann
Art Director Dr. Maria Anna Kollmann
Copywriter Franz Novotny
Designer Franz Novotny
Agency Producer Franz Novotny
Production Company Novotny &
Novotny Film Produktions GmbH

12 **Posters**
Poster Advertising

National Award Gold
Title Herzkurve
Design Studio Heye & Partner GmbH,
Wein
Client McDonald's Austria
Creative Directors Alexander Bartel
Martin Kießling
Art Director Frank Widmann
Copywriters Thorsten Meier
Markus Lange Frank Widmann
Ottward Buchner
Photographer Nico Schmid Burgk

13 Posters
Poster Advertising

National Award Silver
Title At his age, one has to take care of his pension
Agency Ammirati Puris Lintas
Client Allianz Elementar Versicherungs AG
Creative Director Dr. Markus Enzi
Art Director Paul Holcmann
Copywriter Hans Juckel
Designer Astrid Bauer
Photographer Gerhard Heller

14 Posters
Poster Advertising

National Award Silver
Title '80' – if you want to take a look
Agency Demner, Merlicek & Bergmann Ges.m.b.H.
Client Museum für Völkerkunde (Museum of Ethnology)
Creative Director Mariusz Jan Demner
Art Director Elisabeth Sauter
Copywriter Karin Kammlander
Illustrator Elisabeth Sauter
Concept Elisabeth Sauter Karin Kammlander

80 - if you want to take a look. Erotic art from ancient Peru.

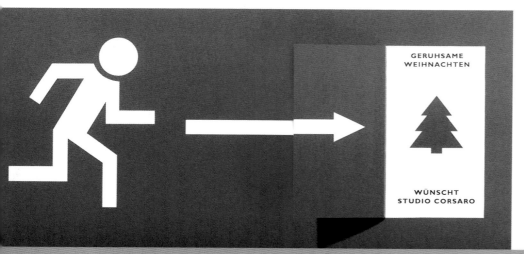

16 Promotion
Mailings

National Award Gold
Title Christmas card
Design Studio Studio Corsaro
Client Studio Corsaro
Creative Director Giovanni Corsaro
Art Director Studio Corsaro
Copywriter Gerry Loibelsberger

15 Promotion
Mailings

National Award Silver
Title Transparent wall
Agency Czerny, Celand, Plakolm
Client Bene Office Furniture
Art Director Gerhard Plakolm
Creative Directors Gerhard Plakolm
Peter Czerny
Copywriter Michael Huber
Designer Markus Göbl

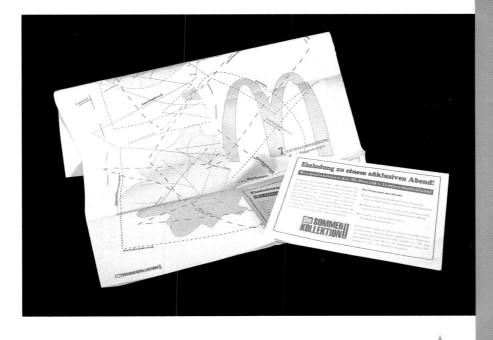

17 Promotion

National Award Gold
Title SA.FE.
Studio Sabine Feichtner
Client Sabine Feichtner
Creative Directors Christoph
Steinegger Sabine Feichtner
Art Director Christoph Steinegger
Designers Sabine Feichtner
Christoph Steinegger
Photographer Elisabeth Grebe

18 Promotion

National Award Silver
Title The summer collection
Agency Heye & Partner Werbeagentur
G.m.b.H.
Client McDonald's Austria
Creative Directors Alexander Bartel
Martin Kießling
Art Director Frank Widmann
Copywriter Florian Nussbaumer

19 Graphic Design

National Award Silver
Title In the edge of time
Design Studio Haslinger, Keck
Client Haslinger, Keck
Creative Director
Hans-Peter Hötzmannseder
Art Directors Christoph Steinegger
Hans-Peter Hötzmannseder
Copywriters Wolfgang Köppel
Norbert Tomasi
Photographer Thomas Smetana

20 Packaging

National Award Silver
Title Nebilet
Design Studio Bárci & Partner
Client Asta Medica Gmbh
Creative Director Peter Kaimer
Art Director Andreas Lierzer

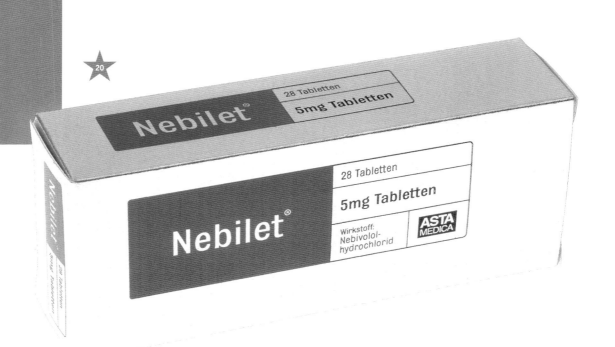

23 **Illustration & Photography**
Illustration

National Award Silver
Title OMV/Research brochure
Agency Lowe/GGK
Client Austrian Mieraloilcompany
Creative Director Chrigel Ott
Art Directors Andreas Berger
Hooman Haghihat
Copywriter Walther Salvenmoser
Illustrator Guy Billout

24 **Illustration & Photography**
Illustration

National Award Gold
Title max. mobil
Design Studio Kutzler & Wimmer
Fotogmbh
Client max. mobil
Telekommunikations GesmbH
Creative Director Dr. Peter Dirnberger
Art Director Michael Heine
Copywriter Ronald Roniger-Kolaczek
Photographer Hannes Kutzler
Illustrator Hannes Kutzler

Whatever you say, it's cheaper from
4pm.

1 **Nomination**
TV & Cinema Advertising
Television Commercial

National Award Gold
Title The longest commercial in the world
Agency McCann Erickson
Client Spaas
Creative Director Tony Hertz
Art Director Michel Derese
Copywriter Jean-Luc Walraff
Advertising Manager Jan Van Cleemput
Account Executives Anita Descheemaeker Joëlle Vandeville
TV Producer Anne Gasia
Production Company MG Productions
Film Director Xavier Harcq
Film Photographer Xavier Harcq

Spaas Festilux Candles don't drip, don't smoke and last longer. And here's the proof.

2 **Nomination**
TV & Cinema Advertising
Television Commercial

National Award Gold
Title Hide and seek
Agency Young & Rubicam Brussels
Client Lotterie National
Creative Director Jean-Paul Bacquer
Art Directors Xavier Boullion Dirk Pierloot
Copywriters Françoise Daubresse Peter Ampe
Advertising Manager Dirk Vercoutter
Account Executive Roger De Henau
TV Producer Eric Peters
Production Company Zia
Film Director Alain Brunard
Music Director Nicolas Fransolet

On Saturday 27 December, you can win 225 million francs with the Lotto. Don't let anyone else win.

3 Nomination
Posters
Poster Advertising

National Award Silver
Title The bat
Agency McCann Erickson
Client Bacardi
Advertising Manager Laurant Jans
Creative Director Tony Hertz
Art Director Eric Vanden Broeck
Copywriter Patrick Pinchart
Account Executive Denis Henet
Photographer Philippe Schmillen

BACARDI
CASA FUNDADA EN SANTIAGO DE CUBA EN 1862

4 Nomination
Promotion
Mailings

National Award Gold
Title Greetings card
Agency Grey Brussels
Client Grey
Advertising Manager Alain Godfroid
Art Director Jan Baert
Copywriter Catherine Quadens
TV Producer Bénédicte Hennen
Production Company Polygone

Enthusiastic reactions from dozens of consumers (both French and Flemish speaking) to vox pop research into a project for a mysterious New Year card, which we never see, because the project is thrown into the bin.
Finale: A little more creativity. A lot less research.

Zeg 'ns A.

koop een klinker.

Notre recette du mois.

Le joystick préféré des créatifs depuis 1984.

5 Print Advertising
Magazine Advertising

National Award Silver
Title A - Class
Agency LdV/Partners
Client Mercedes - Benz
Creative Director Werner Van Reck
Art Director Ivan Moons
Copywriter Stef Selfslagh
Advertising Managers Marc Baddé
Yves Callebaut
Account Executives Colette Pauwels
Beatrice Van Hool
Photographer Rafael Coolen

6 Print Advertising
Trade Advertising

National Award Silver
Title Joystick
Agency VVL/BBDO
Client Apple Macintosh
Creative Director Willy Coppens
Art Director Stephane Abinet
Copywriter Vincent Abrams
Typographer Stephane Abinet
Advertising Manager Christine Gilleir
Account Executive Carola Michiels
Photographer Jean-Pierre Van Der Elst

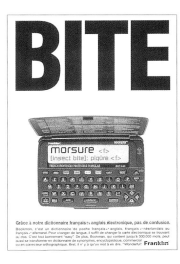

1

2

3

**11 Print Advertising
Newspaper Advertising**

National Award Gold
Title Peugot
Agency Euro RSCG United
Client Peugot Belgium
Creative Director Véronique Hermans
Art Directors Olivier Willems
Claudine Mergaerts
Copywriters Jean-Charles Della Faille
Paul Servais Véronique Hermans
Typographer Joëlle Dumange
Advertising Managers René
Cromphout Eric Elsen

ADCE | Belgium | 30

Account Executives Pierre Mathelart
Bernard Van Oorlé
Photographer Bernard Foubert

1. It's Sunday 8/06. Happy Fathers
Day. (This ad ran on June 8th, Fathers
Day in Belgium).
2. 1st September. Back to school.
Sure, Dad. In the reign of
Charlemagne, kids went to school in a
cart. But that was in AD 806.
3. November 19th, 1997.
Dad, tomorrow the sun rises at 8.06.
A.M. Sweet dreams!
General Endline: Peugeot 806. The car
the kids tell their parents to buy.

**12 Print Advertising
Newspaper Advertising**

National Award Silver
Title The dog
Agency GV/Company
Client De Morgen
Creative Director Bruno Vanspauwen
Art Director Jan Dejonghe
Copywriter Eric Debaene
Typographer Danny Jacquemin
Advertising Manager Koen Clement
Account Executive Inez De Poorter
Photographer Jean-Françoise De
Witte

An extra-thick newspaper. Every
Saturday.

Sadolin
ET LE BOIS EST PLUS FORT

Sadolin makes wood even stronger.

A man in a studio is making the sound effects of a western movie, using usual devices for the sounds of cowboy's actions, and eating a Crac a Nut peanut when the cowboy walks on gravelly soil. Then the man goes on eating, and every action sounds like scrunching crispy peanuts.

15

15 TV & Cinema Advertising
Public Service/Charity

National Award Silver
Title The candle
Agency Bates
Client Amnesty International
Advertising Managers Phillippe
Hensmans Patrick Pauwels
Creative Director Gert Maihieu
Art Director André Plaisier
Copywriter Benoît Menetret
Account Executives Christian Salez
Pascal Kemajou
Production Company Zabriskie
Producer Ann Van Steyvoort
Film Director Patrick Van Hautem
Film Photographer Glynn Speekaert
Music Directors Thierry Plas Doc

Through the bars of a prison, we look
up at the sky.
A bar begins to burn and melt like a
candle, creating an opening towards
the world of the free.
"Each Amnesty International candle
cost 120 francs. The price of
freedom."

16 TV & Cinema Advertising
Cinema Commercial

National Award Gold
Title Fredje
Agency Duval Guillaume
Client BOIC (Belgian Olympic
Committee)
Advertising Manager Piet Moons
Creative Director Guillaume Van Der
Stighelen
Art Director Phillippe De Ceuster
Copywriter Jens Mortier
Account Executive Isabel Peeters
Radio Producer Raf Debraekeleer
Production Company Pix & Motion
Producer Annemie Maes
Film Director Koen Mortier
Film Photographer Glynn Beeckaert

Behind every Olympic champion
there's an Olympic family.

1

2

17 TV & Cinema Advertising
Television Commercial

National Award Silver
Title Diables Rouges
Agency Duval Guillaume
Client UBRSFA
Advertising Manager Jan Peeters
Creative Director
Dominique Van Doormaal
Art Director Alain Janssens
Copywriter Eric Piette
Account Executive Isabel Peeters
Illustrator Denis Courard
TV Producers Raf Debrakeleer
Marc Van Buggenhout
Production Company Blue Stone
Producer Jean-Claude Meert
Film Director Jean-Marc Gerbehaye
Music Whar Zone

Red Devils
1. The Netherlands/Belgium
A Red Devil is holding a piece of
cheese in his hands. He grates this
cheese. A panel announces the football
match Belgium/Holland.
2. Belgium/Wales
A Red Devil is stroking a lamb.
Then he shaves the lamb. A panel
announces the football match
Belgium/Wales.

18 TV & Cinema Advertising
Cinema Commercial

National Award Silver
Title Drosera
Agency BDDP
Client BBL
Advertising Manager
Bruno De Liedekerke
Creative Director Louis Gendebien
Art Director Michel Crabbe
Copywriter Thierry De Caluwe
Typographer Françoise Collignon
Account Executive
Yolande Del Marmol
TV Producers Michel Crabbe
Thierry De Caluwe
Production Company Banana Split
Producer Jean-Luc Van Damme
Film Director Bruno Decharmes
Film Photographer S Leparc
Music Director A Mouysset

**19 TV & Cinema Advertising
Cinema Commercial**

National Award Silver
Title The dog
Agency GV/Company
Client De Morgen
Creative Director Bruno Vanspauwen
Art Director JAn Dejonghe
Copywriter Eric Debaene
Typographer Danny Jacquemin
Account Executive Inez De Pooter
Production Company Blue Stone
Productions
Producer Jean-Claude Meert

An extra thick newspaper. Every
Saturday.

**20 TV & Cinema Advertising
Television Commercial**

National Award Gold
Title Double cheeseburger
Agency Leo Burnett Belgium
Client McDonald's
Creative Director Jean-Luc Soille
Art Director Raymond Gfeller
Copywriter Jean-Luc Soille
Advertising Manager Walter De Groof
Account Executives Stéphane
Buisseret Lena Vynke
TV Producer Monique Sampermans
Production Company Armand
Productions
Film Photographer Nicolas Fransolet
Film Directors Kristiaan Debusscher
Jean-Françoise Julian

Film Photographer Jacques Poskin
Music Director Whar Zone

For 1 coin of 50 Bf, you can get a
double cheeseburger at McDonald's.

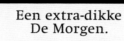

1

Et alors, on fait pipi pendant les pubs?

VESPASIUS

2

Commencez maintenant par un bronze et l'année prochaine faites un gold.

VESPASIUS

21

Eh bien voilà, vous y êtes sur le podium.

VESPASIUS

3

4

Une Clio à 339.000 fb

QUEL AVENIR POUR LES GRANDES?

RENAULT

Une Clio à 339.000 fb

QUEL AVENIR POUR LES GRANDES?

RENAULT

Une Clio à 339.000 fb

QUEL AVENIR POUR LES GRANDES?

RENAULT

22

21 **Posters**
Poster Advertising

National Award Gold
Title Affichettes Gala CCB
Agency Hémisphère Gauche
Client Vespasius
Advertising Managers Christophe Muguerza Hervé Saegaert
Art Director Michel Boudru
Creative Directors Michel Boudru Phillippe Dorval
Copywriter Phillippe Dorval
Typographer Michel Boudru

Posters placed in women's toilets and over urinals during the CCB Gala.

1. Slipped out for a pee during the ads?
2. Start with a bronze now and next year go for gold. (A bronze is slang reference to defecation).
3. There you are, on the platform at last.
4. Make yourself more comfortable. Put your hat here.

22 **Posters**
Poster Advertising

National Award Gold
Title Clio's
Agency Publicis
Client Renault
Advertising Manager Xavier Laporta
Creative Director Marco Calant
Art Director Jean-Marc Wachsmann
Copywriter Gilles De Bruyère
Account Executives Laurent Palmero Madeleine Leclercq
Photographer Hans Kroeskamp

A Clio for 339.000 Fr.
What future does that leave for big cars?

RIEM ECLAT ET LE BOIS REVIT

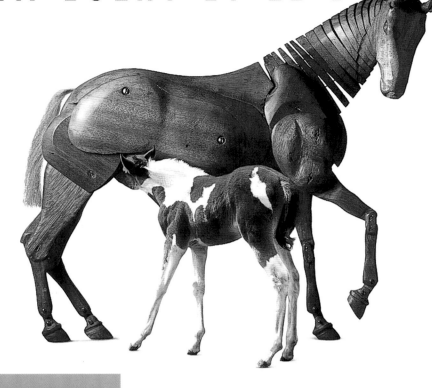

23 Posters
Poster Advertising

National Award Gold
Title The horse
Agency Euro RSCG United
Client Riem
Advertising Managers Emile Nicoletti
Fabrice Nicoletti
Creative Director Véronique Hermans
Art Director Claudine Mergaerts
Copywriter Jean-Charles Della Faille
Account Executive William Lebrun
Photographer Christophe Gilbert

Riem Eclat and the wood comes to life
again.
Riem Eclat restores so much life to
wood, that a foal would mistake a
rocking-horse for its mother.

24 Posters
Poster Advertising

National Award Silver
Title The giant bag
Agency Kadratura
Client Delvaux
Advertising Manager François
Schwennicke
Creative Director Michel Mergaerts
Art Director Sophie Norman
Copywriter Jean-Paul Lefebvre
Account Executive Martine Cosijns

Delvaux is a famous handbag-maker.
The company bought an old house and
asked the agency to conceal the house
until this giant poster was revealed.

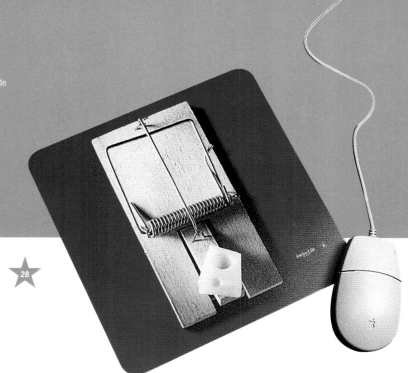

1 Nomination
Graphic Design

National Award Gold
Title Selvsving
Design Studio 2 Graphic Design
Client Danmarks Radio
Creative Directors Jan Nielsen
Ole Lund Jesper Jans T Rosenberg
Photographer Morgan & Morell

2 Print Advertising
Newspaper Advertising

National Award Gold
Title You don't decide where you
are born
Agency Propaganda
Client Information
Creative Director Frederik Preisler
Art Director Hanne Schmidt
Copywriter Frederik Preisler

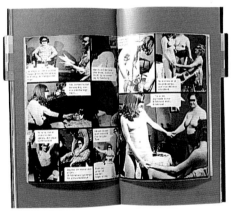

3 Print Advertising
Magazine Advertising

National Award Gold
Title Plungers
Agency McCann Copenhagen
Client Goodyear Denmark
Creative Director Mads Rorstrom
Art Director Robert Cerkez
Copywriter Jesper Hansen
Photographer Klaus Thymann
Account Assistant Christina Boel

4 TV & Cinema Advertising
Television Commercial

National Award Gold
Title Both wheels firmly on the ground
Agency buhl Unltd
Client Everton Smith
Creative Director Dorte Zangenberg
Art Director Dorte Zangenberg
Copywriter Nicolai Stahl
Film Director Kristian Levring
Director of Photography
Jens Schlosse
Production Company Barke, Sonne
& Levring

RØDBY 0,1m. OVER HAVET

AMAGER FÆLLED 1m. OVER HAVET

7 Promotion

National Award Gold
Title Carlsberg beer election
Agency Saatchi & Saatchi A/S
Client Carlsberg Brewery
Creative Director Patrick Isaak
Art Director Claus Fynbo
Copywriter Peter Boye
Photographer Fintan Damgaard

1st candidate, CARLS SPECIAL:
Now the most difficult election in the
history of Denmark begins. The first
candidate is round, golden and already
known in certain circles.
2nd candidate, OLD BOND:
The second candidate of The Beer
Election is ultra-Conservative. Old
Bond is a traditional ale, brewed on
English hops.
3rd candidate, RED X:
The third candidate of The Beer
Election is red. Red X is a fresh 'red
beer' with character, brewed on special
roasted malt.
4th candidate, OTTILIA:
Female vote-puller runs for The Beer
Election '97. Ottilia is a different,
seasoned beer with a seductive
character.
5th candidate, MASTER BREW:
Master Brew runs the election on a
solid basis. Twice as much of
everything and an extremely full-
bodied taste.
6th candidate, CARLSBERG STOUT:
The dark horse of the beer election is
called Carlsberg Stout. A different light
porter with a touch of liquorice.

8 Packaging

National Award Gold
Title Selvsving
Design Studio 2 Graphic Design
Client Danmarks Radio
Creative Directors Jan Nielsen
Ole Lund Jesper Jans T Rosenberg
Photographer Morgan & Morell

9 Illustration & Photography
Illustration

National Award Gold
Title Chair
Design Studio Bates Copenhagen
Client DSB Rails
Creative Director Ib Borup
Art Director Claus Moellebro
Copywriter Jakob Blom
Illustrator Jan Tvilling

You'll be comfortably off.

10 Illustration & Photography
Photography

National Award Gold
Title Exhibit E
Studio Juul & Staehr Photography
Client Rem Rem WP APS Denmark
Art Directors Peter Stenbaek
Claus Skytte
Photographer Martin Juul

Germany

1 **Nomination**
Print Advertising
Magazine Advertising

National Award Gold
Title Frankfurter Allgemeine Zeitung campaign
Agency Scholz & Friends Berlin
Client Frankfurter Allgemeine Zeitung
Creative Director Sebastian Turner
Art Director Petra Reichenbach
Copywriter Sebastian Turner
Graphic Artist Frank Melzer
Photographer Alfred Seiland
Post Production Hans-Jürgen Gaeltzner

1. Ulf Merhold, ESA – Astronaut
2. Vicco Von Bülow, Loriot
3. Yehudi Menuhin
There is always a clever mind behind it.

2 **Nomination**
Graphic Design

National Award Silver
Title Nevertheless posters
Design Studio Uwe Loesch
Client Museum für Kunst & Gewerbe Hamburg/Verlag H Schmidt Mainz
Art Director Uwe Loesch
Designer Gertrud Nolte
Photographer Udo Bechmann

Catalogue of an exhibition of posters by Uwe Loesch.

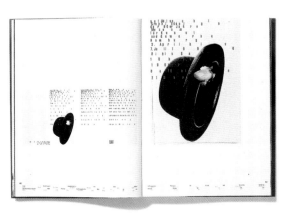
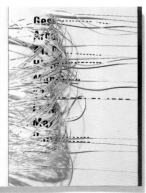

ADCE | Germany | 44

3   Nomination
Illustration & Photography
Photography

National Award Silver
Title Final destination hope
Editors Stern Magazine
Publishing House Gruner & Jahr AG
Photographer Sebastiao Salgado

Bombay, city of dreams for the poor;
Eldorado for smugglers, filmstars, and
textile moguls is on the verge of
collapsing.

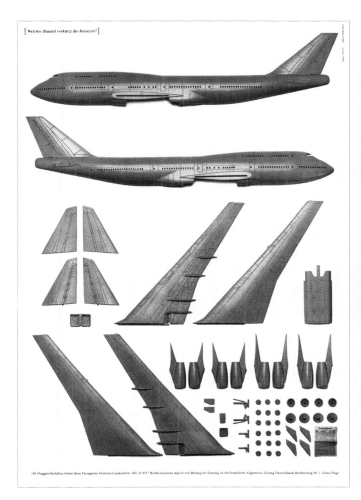

4   Print Advertising
Newspaper Advertising

National Award Silver
Title The inflight newspaper
Agency Scholz & Friends Berlin
Client Frankfurter Allgemeine Zeitung
Creative Director Sebastian Turner
Art Director Raban Ruddigkeit
Copywriters Joachim Schöpfer
Cosima Reif

106 airlines offer their passengers the
best in reading comfort. With 35.953
on-board copies a day from Monday to
Saturday, Frankfurter Allgemeine
Zeitung is Germany's No. 1 in flight
newspaper. Have a good flight.

1   2   3

5 Print Advertising
Newspaper Advertising

National Award Silver
Title Sixt campaign
Agency Jung von Matt Werbeagentur
Client Sixt GmbH & Co
Autovermietung KG
Creative Director Stefan Meske
Art Director Thomas Pakull
Copywriters Stefan Meske
Sebastian Hardieck
Photographers Andreas Burz
Tom Nagy

1. No car rental makes customers
unhappier.
2. If the Finance Minister sees this,
he's bound to introduce a business-trip
pleasure tax.
3. Sixt's Easter message: Don't go to
church! Drive there!

6 Print Advertising
Magazine Advertising

National Award Silver
Title René Lezard campaign
Agency Jung von Matt Werbeagentur
Client René Lezard Mode GmbH
Creative Director
Hermann Waterkamp
Art Director Lars Kruse
Copywriters Ralf Nolting
Doerte Spengler
Photographer Uwe Duettmann

1. Just how long will you wait for
someone to admire you?
2. Your children are the only ones who
really don't mind what you look like.
3. Everybody's an individual. Shame if
you don't notice.

1

UND WIE LANGE WOLLEN SIE NOCH WARTEN,

UM VON JEDEM BEWUNDERT ZU WERDEN?

RENÉ LEZARD
Men's Women's Collection

2

RENÉ LEZARD

3

RENÉ LEZARD

1

2

3

8

2

3

1

7 Print Advertising
Magazine Advertising

National Award Silver
Title Sixt campaign
Agency Jung von Matt Werbeagentur
Client Sixt GmbH & Co
Autovermietung KG
Creative Director Stefan Meske
Art Director Thomas Pakull
Copywriters Stefan Meske
Sebastian Hardieck
Photographers Andreas Burz
Tom Nagy

1. The car for the price of a parking
ticket.
2. Get your pulse racing again.
3. Your wife thinks you're on a
business trip.
And you think your wife's ironing.

8 Print Advertising
Magazine Advertising

National Award Silver
Title Stern Teaser-campaign
Agency KNSK BBDO Werbeagentur
Client Gruner + Jahr AG & Co
Creative Directors Wolfgang Sasse
Beat Nägeli
Art Directors Jürgen Florenz
René Wolf
Copywriter Kai Flemming

1. What's happening in the
World is Stern.
2. What shocks us is in Stern.
3. What turns us on is in Stern.

1

2

3

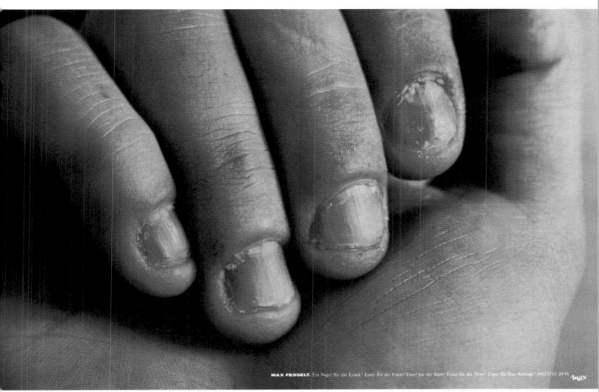

MAX FESSELT. Ein Nagel für die Erotik? Einer für die Fotos? Einer für die Stars? Einer für die News? Einer für Ihre Anzeige? 040/3703-2490

Muß ein Network aussehen wie ein Network?

1

Muß eine Limousine aussehen wie eine Limousine?   Der neue Audi A6. Visionen beginnen mit Fragen.

2

11 Print Advertising
Trade Advertising

National Award Silver
Title Max campaign spring 1997
Agency Baader, Lang, Behnken
Client Gruner + Jahr Verlag
Creative Director Fred Baader
Art Director Andreas Lühmann
Copywriter Henrike Sander
Photographer Uwe Düttmann

1. Max goes really deep. Is it our visual impact? Verbal violence? Our erotic appeal? Or perhaps your advertisement? Who knows?
2. Max provides food for thought. Max feeds minds. Max caters for their needs. Max gives sustinence. Max is appetizing.
3. Max sets them on edge. One nail for erotic appeal? One for the photos? One for the celebrities? One for the news? One for your advertisement?

12 Print Advertising
Trade Advertising

National Award Silver
Title Network
Agency Jung von Matt Werbeagentur
Client Audi AG
Creative Director
Deneke von Weltzien
Art Director Roland Schwarz
Copywriters Sebastian Hardieck
Timm Weber
Photographer Uwe Düttmann

1. Must a network look like a network?
2. Must a saloon look like a saloon? The new Audi A6. Visions start with questions.

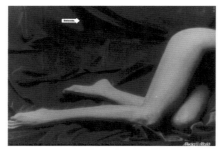

1

2

13 Print Advertising
Trade Advertising

National Award Silver
Title Media Markt campaign
Agency For Sale Werbeagentur GmbH
Client Media Markt Elektro GmbH
Creative Director Kai Fehse
Art Director Jens Jancke
Copywriter Kai Fehse
Designer Jens Jancke

1. Little reminder: There is much more
to life than those stupid computers. So
don't spend too much on them.
Arrow: Raw silk.
2. Little reminder: There is much more
to life than those stupid computers. So
don't spend too much on them.
Arrow: Muschelkalk.
3. Little reminder: There is much more
to life than those stupid computers. So
don't spend too much on them.
Arrow: Centrifugal Forces.

3

14 TV & Cinema Advertising
Television Commercial

National Award Silver
Title Maharaja
Agency Jung von Matt Werbeagentur
Client Audi AG
Creative Director
Hermann Waterkamp
Art Director Uli Guertler
Copywriter Frank Dovidat
Agency Producer Michael Besler
Film Director Zack Snyder
Director of Photography Larry Fong
Production Company Markenfilm

A Maharaja has invited various
ambassadors to a dinner party. Outside
the monsoon is raining and no
ambassador has yet arrived. Suddenly
the Swedish Ambassador rings up to
say he can not come because his car
has got stuck in the monsoon. Then
the British Ambassador's driver rings
to say they are both in hospital after an
accident caused by the torrential rain.
Again the phone rings. This time it's
the German Ambassador calling to say
he will unfortunately be late, he first
has to pick up his Japanese colleague
with his Audi A4.

DER SPIEGEL

TITANIC

SPIEGEL-Leser wissen mehr.

15 TV & Cinema Advertising
Television Commercial

National Award Silver
Title The next generation
Agency Springer & Jacoby Werbung
Client Daimler-Benz AG, Stuttgart
Creative Directors Kurt Georg Dieckert
Stefan Schmidt
Art Director Oliver Haupt
Copywriter Alexander Schill
Agency Producer Natascha Teidler
Film Director Peggy Sirota

Director of Photography Lance Accord
Producer Stephan Fruth
Production Company Neue
Sentimental Film Hamburg

We see children playing. Above a little,
the question: "The next UN Secretary-
General?" is supered in. Another girl
looks up to the sky and we read: "The
first person on Mars?" We see a little
black boy and read: "The future
President of the United States?...We
believe in the next generation." In the
final frames we see an A-class driving
across the picture. Super: "Mercedes
Benz The A-class."

16 Posters
Poster Advertising

National Award Silver
Title Titanic
Agency Springer & Jacoby Werbung
Client Spiegel-Verlag, Hamburg
Creative Directors Kurt Georg Dieckert
Stefan Schmidt
Art Director Axel Thomsen
Photographer Dirk Karsten
Designer Christina Petrich

Spiegel readers know more.

17 Posters
Poster Advertising

National Award Silver
Title Germans out
Agency Jung von Matt Werbeagentur
Client Sixt Travel GmbH
Creative Director Frank Dovidat
Art Director Thomas Pakull
Copywriters Stefan Meske
Dasa Szekely

Reverses the slogan used by German
neo-Nazis: Foreigners out!

18 Posters
Poster Advertising

National Award Silver
Title Key
Agency Grabarz & Partner
Werbeagentur GmbH
Client Ikea Deutschland Verkaufs-
GmbH & Einrichtungs KG
Creative Directors Andreas Grabarz
Mikael Andström
Art Director Derik Meinköhn
Copywriter Ralf Heuel
Designer Derik Meinköhn
Photographer Reinhard Hunger,
Hamburg

Right, straight on, Schnelsen-nord
junction.

Rechts, geradeaus,
Abfahrt Schnelsen-Nord.

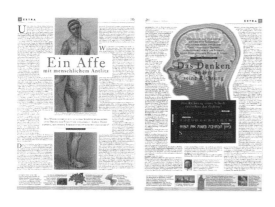

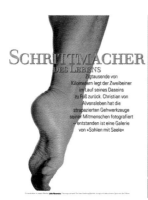

1

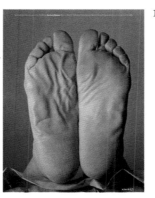

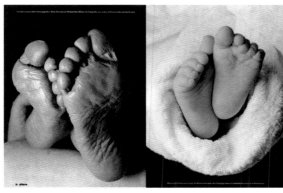

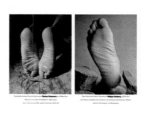

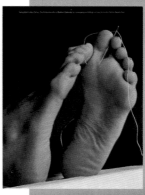

2   3

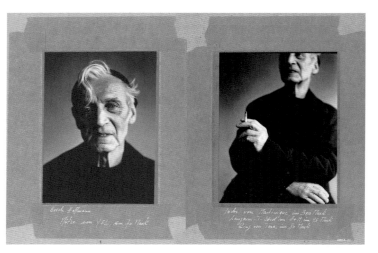

21 Editorial

National Award Silver
Title When I'm eighty four
Publishing House AMICA Verlag
GmbH & Co KG
Editor in Chief Ulla Hildebrand
Art Directors Helmut Kruse
Heico Forster
Design Director Hans-Jürgen Polster
Designer Hans-Jürgen Polster
Photographer Matthias Ziegler
Calligrapher Matthias Ziegler
Booking Editor Beka Kammann
Photo Director Carola Born
Fashion Director Christiane Arp

They are cool. They sparkle with temperament. They enjoy life. For AMICA women and men between the ages of 57 to 84 took part in a photo-shoot wearing designer fashion. Look at the photos and you will find that compared to them most young people would look "old".

22 Illustration & Photography
Illustration

National Award Gold
Title Culture-sponsoring
Design Studio Inkognito
Client Inkognito
Creative Director Michael Etter
Illustrator Gerhard Glück

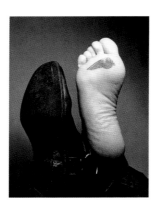 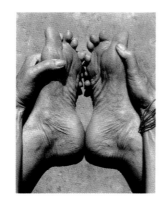 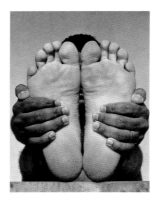

25 Illustration & Photography
Photography

National Award Silver
Title Soles soul or pacemaker of life
Studio Atelier Christian von Alvensleben
Photographer Christian von Alvensleben

26 Illustration & Photography
Photography

National Award Silver
Title There is always a clever mind behind it
Agency Scholz & Friends Berlin
Client Frankfurter Allgemeine Zeitung GmbH
Creative Director Sebastian Turner
Art Director Petra Reichenbach
Copywriter Sebastian Turner
Graphic Artist Frank Melzer
Photographer Alfred Seiland
Post Production Hans-Jürgen Gaeltzner

"The Internet is full of inspiration for the creative mind. Great new ways of killing greenfly, for instance."

John Rocha, fashion designer and gardener.

John's Top Websites

Visiting a gardening website. E-mailing fellow enthusiasts about organic pest control. Finding out what words like 'website' and 'e-mail' actually mean.

All made possible by Telecom Internet. We've got all the resources you need to get the most out of the Internet. Including Doras, the world's most comprehensive directory of Irish-interest sites.

And we've got a seven day help desk

So if you want to get started
CALLSAVE 1850 203 204

TELECOM INTERNET: www.tinet.ie

1   **Print Advertising**
    Newspaper Advertising

    National Award Silver
    Title John Rocha
    Agency McConnells
    Client Telecom Eireann
    Concepts Paudge Donaghy
    Laurence Keogh
    Art Director Paudge Donaghy
    Copywriter Laurence Keogh
    Designer/Typography Paudge Donaghy
    Laurence Keogh
    Photographer Trevor Hart

2   **Print Advertising**
    Newspaper Advertising

    National Award Silver
    Title Fly
    Agency Des O'Meara & Partners
    Client Unitherm
    Art Director Ciara Winkelmann
    Copywriter Alan Kelly
    Designer Ciara Winkelmann
    Illustrator Ciara Winkelmann

1998 - 1998

HIS DEATH CAME AS A COMPLETE SHOCK.

IF IT FLIES - IT DIES

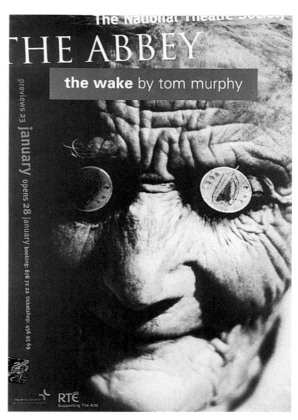

4 Graphic Design

National Award Silver
Title ESB Environmental Review
Design Studio Creative Inputs
Client ESB
Designer Amanda Brady
Illustrator Amanda Brady

3 Posters
Poster Advertising

National Award Gold
Title The Wake
Design Studio Design Works
Client Abbey Theatre
Designer Gene Cooke

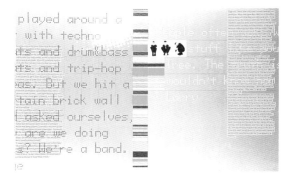

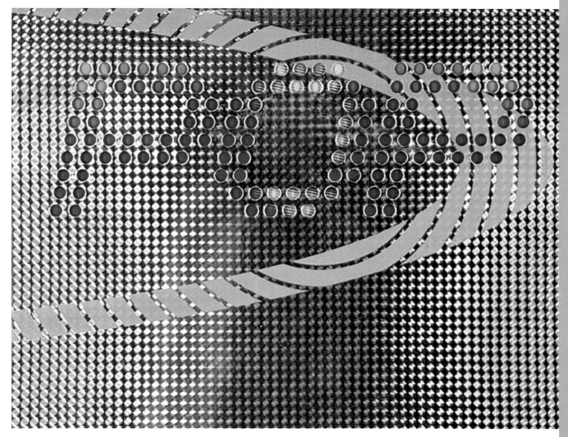

5 Graphic Design

National Award Silver
Title Pop Tour Programme
Design Studio Averill Brophy &
Associates
Client Remind Limited
Art Director Steve Averill
Copywriters Bill Flanagan
Catherine Owens
Designer Shaughn McGrath
Illustrator Shaughn McGrath

6 Graphic Design
Corporate Identity

National Award Silver
Title Design Week Identity
Design Studio Imagenow
Client Institute of Designers of Ireland
Designer David Torpey
Photographer Hugh Glynn
Illustrator David Torpey

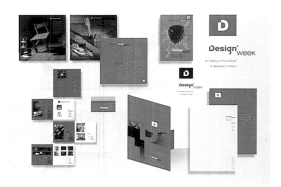

7   Illustration & Photography
Photography

National Award Silver
Title John Rocha
Studio Trevor Hart
Client Telecom Eireann
Art Director Paudge Donaghy
Copywriter Laurence Keogh
Designer Paudge Donaghy
Photographer Trevor Hart

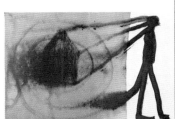

1   Gold
Illustration & Photography
Illustration

National Award Gold
Title Ordinary People
Studio Studio Falavigna
Client Ordinary People
Creative Director Ciro Falavigna
Art Director Ciro Falavigna
Copywriter Chiara Broggi
Illustrator Sandro Fabbri

Italy

2   Nomination
TV & Cinema Advertising
Television Commercial

National Award Gold
Title The challenge
Agency Pirella Göttsche Lowe
Client Supergra
Creative Director Roberto Pizzigoni
Art Director Roberto Pizzigoni
Copywriter Pino Rozzi
Agency Producer Franco Cipolla
Film Director Tarsem
Director of Photography Paul Laufer
Production Company BRW & Partners

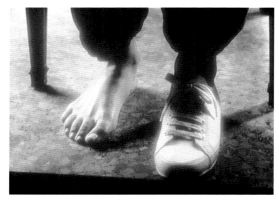

3 Print Advertising
Public Service/Charity

National Award Silver
Title Lapidi
Agency Reggio Del Bravo Pubblicità
Client Ministero Lavori Pubblici
Creative Director Paolo Del Bravo
Art Director Miriam Bianchi
Copywriter Paolo Del Bravo
Photographer Francesco Ferrari
Creative Director Agostino Reggio
Art Director Agostino Reggio

4 Print Advertising
Magazine Advertising

National Award Gold
Title Ku Klux Klan
Agency Saatchi & Saatchi
Client Allied Dunbar
Creative Directors Guido Cornara
Agostino Toscana
Art Directors Agostino Toscana
G Pagliarulo

Unicum. Bevilo se sei un uomo.

5 Print Advertising
Magazine Advertising

National Award Silver
Title Piloti
Agency Young & Rubicam
Client Italiana Petroli
Creative Directors Salvo Mizzi
Antonio Vignali
Art Director Filippo Magri
Copywriter Andrea Ruggeri
Photographer Tony Thorimbert

6 Print Advertising
Trade Advertising

National Award Gold
Title Fiori
Agency BBDO Italia
Client Henkel
Creative Director Daniele Cima
Art Director Chiara Giasolli
Copywriter Renzo Mati
Photographer Marco Ambrosi

Mercurio Cinematografica has decided to change its logo. Those against, please raise their hands.

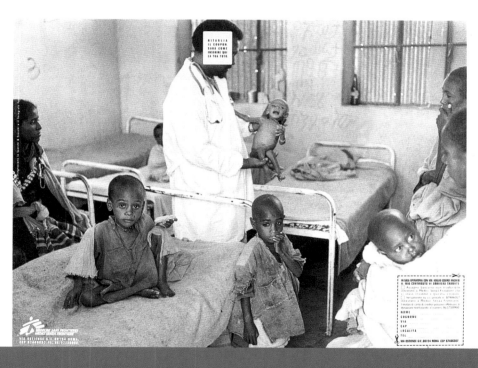

7   **Print Advertising**
    Trade Advertising

    National Award Silver
    Title Ammazzato
    Agency GNAF
    Client Mercurio Cinematografica
    Art Director Giorgio Natale
    Copywriter Federica Ariangio
    Photographer Paolo Pagani

8   **Print Advertising**
    Public Service/Charity

    National Award Gold
    Title Foto Tessera
    Agency Saatchi & Saatchi
    Client Medici Senza Frontiere
    Creative Directors Luca Albanese
    Stefano Maria Palombi
    Art Director Luca Albanese
    Photographer Ferdinando Scianna-
    Magnum
    Production Company Livia Pompili
    Copywriter Stefano Maria Palombi

9,10 Print Advertising
Newspaper Advertising

National Award Gold
National Award Silver
Title Coppa del Mondi di Sci
Agency Publicis
Client Industrie Poretti
Creative Director Maurizio Badiani
Art Director Daniele Ricci
Copywriter Mauro Manieri
Photographer Jean Bernard Aegerter

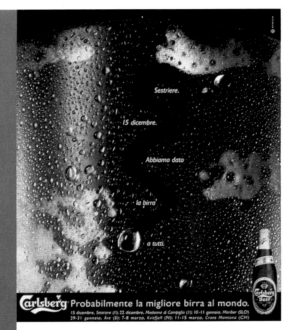

11 TV & Cinema Advertising
Television Commercial

National Award Silver
Title Volkswagen Golf "Social
Campaign"
Agency Verba DDB
Client Autogerma
Creative Directors Gianfranco
Marabelli Erinco Bonomimi
Art Director Marcello Porta
Copywriter Alessandro Omini
Director of Photography
Damien Morisot
Film Director Alek Keshishian
Agency Producers Guiseppe Brandolini
Simona Butta
Production Company Film Master

12 TV & Cinema Advertising
Television Commercial

National Award Gold
Title Beach
Agency BBH/Selection
Client Perfetti SPA Italy
Creative Director Steve Hooper
Art Director Mike Wells
Copywriter Will Burnett
Agency Producer Susan Vale
Film Director Harald Zwart
Production Company
The Pink Film Company

13 TV & Cinema Advertising
Television Commercial

National Award Gold
Title Goddess – Marie José-Perec
Agency Young & Rubicam
Client Pirelli Spa
Creative Director Gerard De Thame
Art Director Mark Edwards
Copywriter Juoly Kingsley
Agency Producer Young & Rubicam
Film Director Gerard De Thame
Director of Photography Russel
Porads
Production Company Gerard De
Thame Films

Power is nothing without control. New
Pirelli Drago.

14 Posters
Poster Advertising

National Award Silver
Title Mani
Agency Saatchi & Saatchi
Client Honda
Creative Directors Luca Albanese
Stefano Maria Palombi
Art Director Luca Albanese
Copywriter Stefano Maria Palombi
Photographer Riccardo Abbondanza

15 Posters
Poster Advertising

National Award Gold
Title Walnut
Agency Pirella Göttsche Löwe
Client Volvo
Creative Directors Roberto Pizzigoni
Aldo Cernuto
Photographer Maurizio Cigognetti

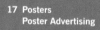

16 Posters
Poster Advertising

National Award Silver
Title MTV
Agency Pirella Göttsche Löwe
Client MTV
Creative Director Emanuele Pirella
Art Director Roberto Battaglia
Copywriter Pino Rozzi
Photographer Valerio De Berardinas

17 Posters
Poster Advertising

National Award Gold
Title Goalkeepers
Agency Wieden & Kennedy
Client Nike
Creative Director Jon Matthews
Art Director Bertrand Fleuret
Copywriter Lorenzo De Rita

Dei limiti di velocità se n'è sempre sbattuto.

Rispetta il Codice della Strada. Rispetta il valore della vita. MINISTERO DEI LAVORI PUBBLICI
Ispettorato Generale per la Circolazione e la Sicurezza Stradale

Con una mano fumava, con l'altra telefonava e con l'altra guidava.

Rispetta il Codice della Strada. Rispetta il valore della vita. MINISTERO DEI LAVORI PUBBLICI
Ispettorato Generale per la Circolazione e la Sicurezza Stradale

Ragazzi quando bevo mi gira tutto.

Rispetta il Codice della Strada. Rispetta il valore della vita. MINISTERO DEI LAVORI PUBBLICI
Ispettorato Generale per la Circolazione e la Sicurezza Stradale

18 Posters
Poster Advertising

National Award Gold
Title Valore Della Vita
Agency Reggio Del Bravo Pubblicità
Client Ministero Lavori Pubblici
Creative Directors Paolo Del Bravo
Agostino Reggio
Copywriter Paolo Del Bravo
Photographer Alessandro Valeri

19 Graphic Design

National Award Gold
Title 161 PIX
Design Studio Smith Family
Client Andrea Pizzi
Designers Miriam Bianchi
Fabio Giannotti

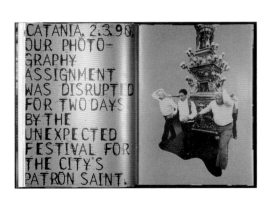

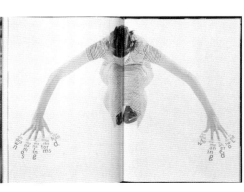

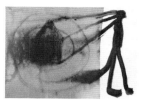

20 Graphic Design

National Award Silver
Title Varide Cicognany corporate identity
Design Studio Matite Giovanotte
Client Varide Cicognani
Creative Director Giovanni Pizzigati
Art Director Giovanni Pizzigati
Designer Giovanni Pizzigati

21 Graphic Design

National Award Gold
Title Ordinary People
Design Studio Studio Falavigna
Client Ordinary People
Creative Director Ciro Falavigna
Art Director Ciro Falavigna
Copywriter Michela Gattermayer
Designer Chiara Broggi
Illustrator Sandro Fabbri

24 Editorial

National Award Gold
Title 161 PIX
Design Studio Smith Family
Client Andrea Pizzi
Designers Miriam Bianchi
Fabio Giannotti

25 Editorial

National Award Silver
Title Cuba
Design Studio Cento Per Cento
Client Rizzoli
Creative Director Pier Paolo Pitacco
Photographer Eddy Kohli

C U B A

24

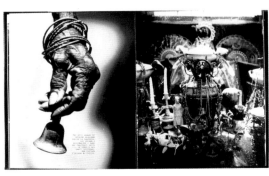

25

1   Gold
    Print Advertising
    Magazine Advertising

    National Award Silver
    Title Safety on board
    Agency TBWA/Campaign Company
    Client Samsonite Europe NV
    Art Directors Arjan van Woensel
    Ferry van Tongeren
    Copywriters Arjan van Woensel
    Ferry van Tongeren
    Photographer Carlfried Verwaayen
    Illustrators Arjan van Woensel
    Ferry van Tongeren

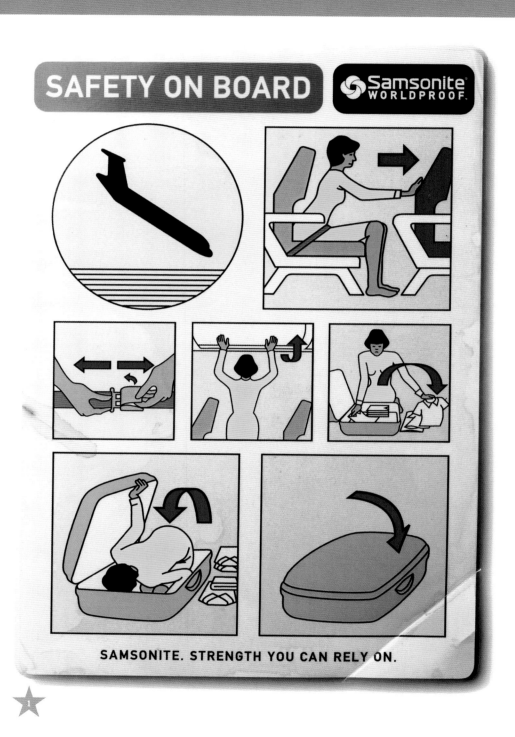

AvPlu

Chapter Five
Vijfde Hoofdstuk

In which mention is made of a Moving Floor, an Indian
Summer Christmas tree and Twenty-five Identical Clocks

Waarin sprake is van een Bewegende Vloer, een
Nazomer-kerstboom en Vijfentwintig Identieke Klokken

'Hier wordt de spot gedreven met de heiligste gevoelens van een
groot deel van het Nederlandse Volk. Wordt het geen tijd dat de minister het te weten komt? Anders moeten de kerken er maar iets aan gaan
doen!' words were spoken by the Reverend L.L. Blok and were
Bovenstaande regels zijn van dominee L.L. Blok. Ze werden in het
najaar van 1969 afgedrukt in het krantje 'Hervormd Amsterdam'.
Het ging ditmaal niet om een kwetsend tv-programma, maar om een
kunstwerk. Een tijdelijk kunstwerk van Wim T. Schippers.
In september 1969 verrees aan het Amsterdamse Leidseplein, vlak
voor Americain, een groot formaat kerstboom, fraai opgetuigd met
slingers en ballen. Er was een grijze vlag naast gezet, maar die viel
wat minder op. Eigenlijk was het de bedoeling dat de naaldboom
midden in de zomer zou worden geïnstalleerd, maar dat werd als wer-
kelijk misplaatst beschouwd; september kon nog net. 'In fantasieloos
Rotterdam of Den Haag zou zo'n voorstel natuurlijk terstond van de
hand zijn gewezen. Zo echter niet in het pulserend, swingend
Amsterdam', mopperde Het Vrije Volk.
Twee jaar later was het Rembrandtsplein aan de beurt. In het zomerse
gazon werden vijfentwintig identieke stadsklokken neergezet, die ook
allemaal dezelfde tijd aangaven. Verder werd het plein opgesierd met
vierentwintig lichtbakken die de richting aangaven naar onder meer
'Darkanivap', 'Bugpeh', 'Knetten', 'Driehelb' en 'AvPlu'. Sommige
mensen vonden het wel aardig, maar bij anderen veroorzaakte het project verwarring en woede. Zo werd er veel geklaagd over de zinloos-
heid ervan – 'ze lijken wel gek bij de gemeente' – en het vele 'verspilde'
geld dat ermee gemoeid zou zijn. Dat laatste viel overigens wel mee,
want er was gewerkt met bestaand materiaal en na afloop, eind september, waren de klokken weer op andere plaatsen te gebruiken.

Kennelijk mag kunst wel wat kosten, maar dan moet het er ook als
zodanig uitzien. In elk plantsoen staat wel een beeld. Ook in het
38 Amsterdamse water drijft veel kunst. Artistiek vormgegeven 'lichtlij-

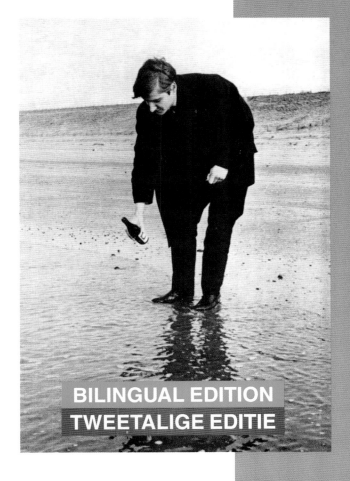

BILINGUAL EDITION
TWEETALIGE EDITIE

2 **Gold**
Graphic Design

National Award Silver
Title The best of Wim T. Schippers
Studio Studio Gonnissen en
Widdershoven
Client Centraal Museum Utrecht
Art Directors Nikki Gonnissen
Thomas Widdershoven
Copywriter Harry Ruhé
Designers Nikki Gonnissen
Thomas Widdershoven

3 Nomination
TV & Cinema Advertising
Television Commercial

National Award Silver
Title Daytrip
Agency PMSvW/Young & Rubicam
Client Soesman Language Training
Creative Director Karel Beyen
Art Director Rob van Gijzelen
Copywriter Maurice van Gijzelen
Agency Producer Marijke Kolsteeg
Film Directors Matthias Schut
Laurence Hamburger
Production Company CCCP.Com

Grandparents take their two
grandchildren (girls) for a ride. They
get in the car and the radio pops on.
We hear the following lyric: "I wanna
fuck you in the arse". The reaction on
the faces shows that they like the tune.
They wiggle their heads to the rhythm
of the song. The little girls in the back
also wiggle their heads.
Then a super appears:
Wanna learn English? Followed by:
Soesman Language Training.

4 Nomination
TV & Cinema Advertising
Television Commercial

National Award Silver
Title The commentary/The eagle
Agency Wieden & Kennedy
Amsterdam
Client Coca Cola
Creative Director Jon Matthews
Art Director Ollie Watson
Copywriters Nick Wray
Ollie Watson
Agency Producer Tim Maguire
Film Director Leonard Dorfman
Production Company Radical Media

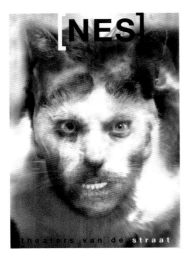 

5 Nomination
Illustration & Photography
Illustration

National Award Silver
Title Theatre posters
Design Studio Laboratorivm
Client Stichting Nes Theaters
Photographer (Dog poster) Wim van der Hulst

Streetwise theatres. Nes is the name of collective well known theatres who are based in one street called Nes.

6 Print Advertising
Newspaper Advertising

National Award Silver
Title Push-ups
Agency TBWA/Campaign Company
Client Telfort
Art Director Diederick Hillenius
Copywriter Poppe van Pelt
Photographer Paul Ruigrok

Just a year old, but already in great shape. Telfort. The combined experience of British Telecom and Dutch Railways.

7   TV & Cinema Advertising
    Television Commercial

    National Award Gold
    Title 'Motorcycle'
    Agency Lowe Kuiper & Schouten
    Client Melkunie BV
    Creative Directors Aad Kuijper
    Pieter van Velsen
    Art Director Pieter van Velsen
    Copywriter Aad Kuijper
    Designer Adrian Walton Smith
    Agency Producer Peter Burger
    Film Director Hans van Rijs
    Director of Photography Joost van
    Starrenburg
    Production Company Ocean View

    Melkunie Milkshake 'Motorcyle'.

8   TV & Cinema Advertising
    Television Commercial

    National Award Gold
    Title For real players only
    Agency Result DDB
    Client De Lotto
    Art Director Jeroen van Zwam
    Copywriter Marcel Hartog
    Agency Producers Yolande van der
    Meulen Wies Verbeek
    Film Director Rick Lenzing
    Director of Photography Steve Walker
    Production Company Cellusion Films

    Toto Select "For real players only".

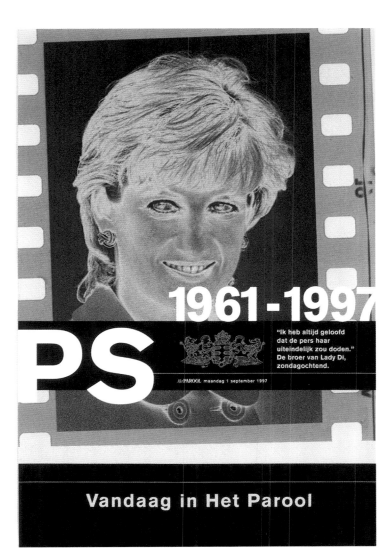

11

12

11 Promotion
Mailings

National Award Silver
Title Belief in advertising
Agency KesselsKramer
Client Het Parool
Creative Directors Erik Kessels
Johan Kramer
Art Director Erik Kessels
Copywriters Franklin Neuteboom
Johan Kramer
Designer Erik Kessels
Photographer Jose Groot

12 Promotion

National Award Gold
Title Dream Green
Agency KesselsKramer
Client Nike Europe
Creative Directors Erik Kessels
Johan Kramer
Art Director Erik Kessels
Copywriters Tyler Whisnand
Johan Kramer
Illustrator Erik Kessels

1

2

3

4

5

 13

13 **Editorial**

National Award Silver
Title Come and see this!, Talk Radio, Hamlet, Cuba crisis, XTC, Scandals in the Hague
Agency KesselsKramer
Client Het Parool
Creative Directors Erik Kessels
Johan Kramer
Art Directors Erik Kessels
Harmine Louwé
Copywriters Johan Kramer
Matthys Van Hieuwkerk
Designer Harmine Louwé
Photographer Simon Larbalestier
Illustrator Stang

1. Come and see this
2. Talk radio
3. Cuba Crisis
4. XTC
5. Scandals in the Hague

14 **Illustration & Photography**
Photography

National Award Silver
Title Two Dogs/Beware
Agency Garbergs Amsterdam
Client Bols Benelux
Art Directors Mark Aink
Remco Bos
Copywriters Paul Falla
Dennis Zijlstra
Photographer J.K. Potter

 14

Norway

1 Gold
Promotion

National Award Silver
Title Yves Klein exhibition
Agency Bold Advertising
Client The National Museum of
Contemporary Art
Art Director Stephanie Dumont
Copywriter Fred Hauge

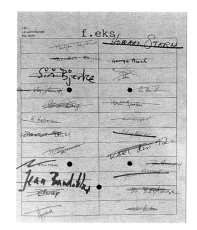

2 Nomination
Editorial

National Award Gold
Title F.eks magazine
Design Studio Geir Henriksen Design
Studio/Astronaut
Client F.eks
Art Director Geir Henriksen
Designers Lars Gulliksen Aina Griffin
Geir Henriksen
Photographers Lars Gulliksen
Aina Griffin Geir Henriksen
Illustrators Lars Gulliksen Aina Griffin
Geir Henriksen

3 Nomination
Posters
Poster Advertising

National Award Silver
Title New members for a sports club
Agency Bates Benjamin
Client Ullern Basketball Club
Art Director Tor Alf Elverum
Copywriter Tor Bertheussen

4   Nomination
     Illustration & Photography
     Illustration

     National Award Gold
     Title And it was Cain who killed Abel
     Client Klassekampen
     Designer Heidi Aspli
     Illustrator Trude Tjensvold

**5 Print Advertising
Magazine Advertising**

National Award Silver
Title Side impact
Agency Bates Backer
Client Harald A Møller
Art Director Thorbjørn Naug
Copywriter Aris Theophilakis

**6 Print Advertising
Magazine Advertising**

National Award Silver
Title Torn paper, Paper plane,
Side impact
Agency Bates Backer
Client Harald A Møller
Art Director Thorbjørn Naug
Copywriter Aris Theophilakis

Sidekollisjonsputer er standard

Alt du ikke trenger til faste høye priser

TATLER

11 Print Advertising
Newspaper Advertising

National Award Silver
Title Tarzan
Agency Bates Camp
Client Oslo Gay & Lesbian Festival
Art Director Anne Gravingen
Copywriter Bendik Romstad
Illustrator Bjørn Brochmann

Me Tarzan you John.

12 TV & Cinema Advertising
Public Service / Charity

National Award Gold
Title Telethon
Agency Schjelderup-Lund, Bendixen & Partners
Client The Norwegian Cancer Society
Creative Director Harald Schjelderup-Lund
Art Director Jørgen Grann
Copywriter Harald Schjelderup-Lund
Agency Producer Tom Jordsjø
Film Director Marius Holst
Director of Photography J C Rosenlund
Production Company Moland Film

13 TV & Cinema Advertising
Television Commercial

National Award Silver
Title Buying a car
Agency JBR Reklamebyrå AS
Client Den Norske Bank
Art Director Eivind Solberg
Copywriter Frode Karlberg
Agency Producer Torleif Hauge
Film Director Lisa Ohlin
Director of Photography
Gaute Gunnari
Production Company JBR Film

14 TV & Cinema Advertising
Television Commercial

National Award Silver
Title Guru
Agency Leo Burnett
Client Thorn
Copywriters Eirik Hovland
Erik Hersoug
Agency Producers Espen Horn
Rickard Ulfengren
Film Director Sam Larsson
Production Company Leo film/Traktor

DAGEN ER IKKE
HELT DEN
SAMME
UTEN VG

Du trenger ikke
pugge alt på en gang.

De blå ordbøkene

Tillatt ved eksamen
i videregående

KUNNSKAPSFORLAGET

15 TV & Cinema Advertising
Television Commercial

National Award Gold
Title The park
Agency New Deal DDB
Client VG
Agency Producer Turid Øversveen
Art Director Ingvar Moi
Copywriter Ivar Vereide
Film Director Hans Petter Moland
Production Company Big Deal Film

16 TV & Cinema Advertising
Television Commercial

National Award Silver
Title Boy
Agency JBR Reklamebyrå AS
Client Kunnskaps Forlaget
Art Director Einar Fjøsne
Copywriter Kjetil Try
Agency Producer Torleif Hauge
Film Director Erik Poppe
Director of Photography
Halvard Breien
Production Company JBR Film
Advertiser's supervisor
Harald Stroemme

17 TV & Cinema Advertising
    Television Commercial

National Award Silver
Title Buss, Fly, Pol, Restaurant,
Liquor Store
Agency JBR Reklamebyrå
Client Kunnskaps Forlaget
Art Director Einar Fjøsne
Copywriter Kjetil Try
Agency Producer Torleif Hauge
Film Director Erik Poppe
Producer JBR Film
Director of Photography
Halvard Breien

You don't have to learn everything
at once.

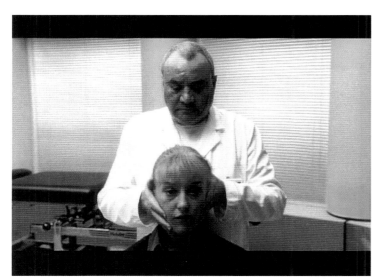

18 TV & Cinema Advertising
    Television Commercial

National Award Silver
Title Kiropraktor
Agency Leo Burnett
Client VW Golf
Art Director Pål Wehus
Copywriter Erik Heisholt
Agency Producer Espen Horn
Film Director Ubbe Haavind
Production Company Leo Film

Audi A4

19 Posters
Poster Advertising

National Award Silver
Title Paper plane
Agency Bates Backer
Client Harald A Møller
Art Director Thorbjørn Naug
Copywriter Aris Theophilakis

20 Posters
Poster Advertising

National Award Gold
Title The kiss
Agency Saatchi & Saatchi
Client Henie Onstad Kunstsenter
Art Director Frode J Karlsen
Photographer Jo Michael

National Award Silver
Title Urgent action
Agency Bates Binders
Client Amnesty International Norway
Art Directors Kjell Ramsdal
Anita Brekke
Designers Anita Brekke Kjell Ramsdal
Photographer Marit Mollnes

National Award Silver
Title Hydrant, Butcher, Postman, Cat
Agency Kontoret -AS Reklamebyrå
Client Vincompagniet
Art Director Knut Pøethe
Copywriter Pål Sparre-Enger
Designer Kurt Haugen
Illustrator Autografene

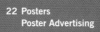

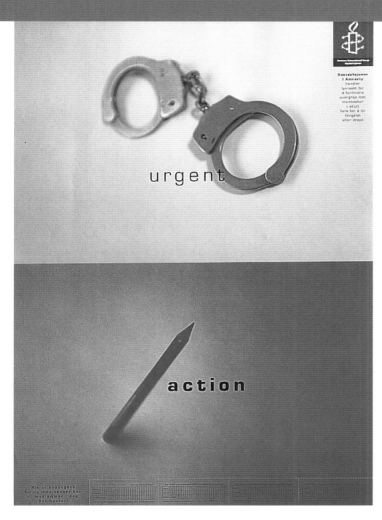

23 Posters
Poster Advertising

National Award Gold
Title Tarzan, Superman,
Mr. Robinson, Freud
Agency Bates Camp
Client Oslo Gay & Lesbian Festival
Art Director Anne Gravingen
Copywriter Bendik Romstad
Illustrator Bjørn Brochmann

24 Promotion

National Award Silver
Title By-Larm
Design Studio Union Design
Client By Larm
Designer Union Design
Illustrator Union Design

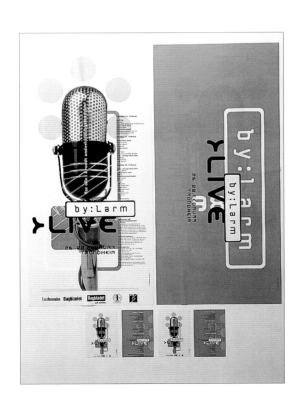

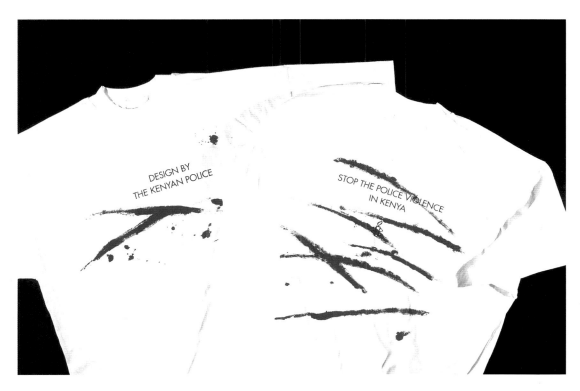

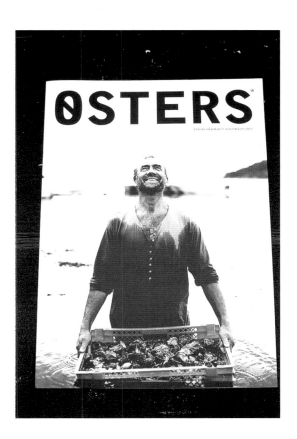

27 Promotion
Mailings

National Award Silver
Title Crop '97
Agency New Deal DDB
Client Reklamefotografenes Forening
(Adv. Photographers Ass.)
Art Director Henrik Sæther
Copywriter Steinar Borge

28 Promotion

National Award Silver
Title The Gate
Design Studio Arne Kaupang
Design AKD
Client The Gate/Zone Productions
Designer Arne Kaupang

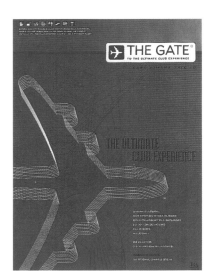

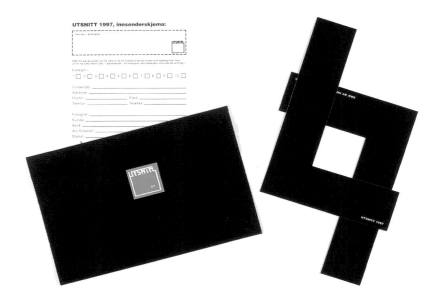

29 Graphic Design

National Award Silver
Title Annual Report
Design Studio Bergsnov, Mellbye &
Rosenbaum AS
Client Orkla Finans AS
Designer Anne Mellbye
Photographer Hoffmanns

30 Graphic Design

National Award Silver
Title A year with Ivar
Design Studio Fasett
Client Ivar - Regional Water Sewage
and Disposal Company
Art Director Trond Fernblad
Designer Trond Fernblad

31 **Graphic Design**
Corporate Identity

National Award Gold
Title TTS
Design Studio Rose & Hopp
Design A/S
Client TTS
Designers Gina Rose Magne Hopp

32 **Packaging**

National Award Gold
Title Gøy packaging
Design Studio Nordahl & Jøntvedt
Design and Illustration
Client Publicis TNT/Stabburet
Art Director Terje Jacobsen
Designer Trond Nordahl
Illustrator Trond Nordahl

33 Illustration & Photography
Illustration

National Award Silver
Title The Phillip's magazine
Design Studio Boge Illustration
Client Phillips Petroleum Company
Norway
Art Director Eirik Moe
Designer Eirik Moe
Illustrator Bjørn Mike Boge

34 Illustration & Photography
Illustration

National Award Silver
Title Annual Report
Design Studio Cox Kommunikasjon
Client KLP Insurance Company
Illustrator Svein Størksen

35 Illustration & Photography
Illustration

National Award Gold
Title Arrow
Design Studio Nordahl & Jøntvedt
Design and Illustration
Client Federation of Norwegian
Process and Manufacturing Industry
Designers T Nordahl A M Solheim
J Jøntvedt
Illustrators A M Solheim T Nordahl

36 Illustration & Photography
Illustration

National Award Silver
Title Piano bar
Design Studio Reklameverkstedet
Client Garman Piano Bar
Art Director Kristian Høiland
Illustrator Finn Graff

 35

36

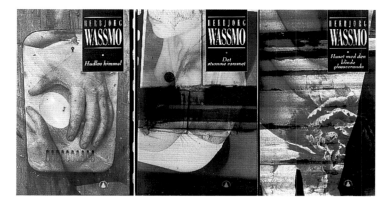

37 Illustration & Photography
Illustration

National Award Gold
Title Book jackets
Client Gyldendal Norsk Forlag
Designer Kristin S Smith
Photographer Liv Andrea Mosdøl
Illustrator Liv Andrea Mosdøl

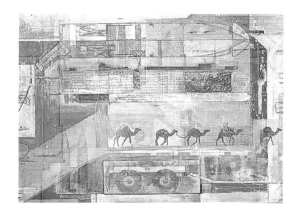

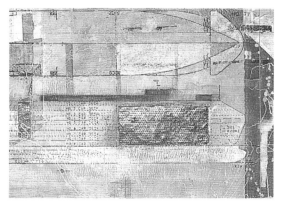

38 Illustration & Photography
Illustration

National Award Gold
Title Annual Report
Design Studio Nordahl & Jøntvedt
Design and Illustration
Client Wilhelm Wilhelmsen
Designed by Nordahl & Jøntvedt
Design and Illustration
Illustrator Anne-Ma Solheim

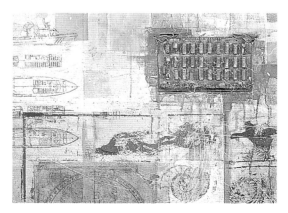

...og tørsten.

Hva er mat?
Er mat kunst?
Er mat livsgnist?
Er mat godt?
Er mat lykken?
Er mat livet?
JA!

39 Illustration & Photography
Illustration

National Award Gold
Title Annual report 1996
Design Studio Bates Binders
Client Smedvig
Art Director Kjell Ramsdal
Designer Kjell Ramsdal
Photographers Yann Aker
Dag Myrestrand
Illustrator Trond Nordahl

40 Illustration & Photography
Photography

National Award Gold
Title Taste
Agency Bates Binders
Client J W Cappelens Forlag A/S
Art Director Kenneth Hansen
Designer Kenneth Hansen
Photographer Knut Bry

41 **Illustration & Photography**
Illustration

National Award Silver
Title Presentation brochure
Agency Bates Binders
Client Conoco
Art Director Kristin Koll Svensen
Designer Kristin Koll Svensen
Illustrator Stein Løken

42 **Illustration & Photography**
Photography

National Award Silver
Title Brochure
Photographer Bjørn-Eivind Årtun
Client Noraqua
Photographer Bjørn-Eivind Årtun
Art Director Kåre Mongstad

43 Illustration & Photography
Illustration

National Award Silver
Title Genetically modified foods
Client Statens Naerngsmiddel Tilsyn
Designer Ellen Jacobson/
Cox Kommunikasjon
Illustrator Anne Kristin Hagesaether

44 Illustration & Photography
Illustration

National Award Silver
Title The Pilgrim's Handbook
Client Verbum (publisher)
Designer Svein Størksen
Illustrator Anne Kristin Hagesaether

PoesiaMúsica

L'Eix uneix Vic i Manresa com mai.

Miquel Martí i Pol i Manel Camp

1   Print Advertising
Public Service/Charity

National Award Gold
Title L'Eix Uneix
Agency Nogué & Cia
Design Studio David Espluga
Marc Ros Nogué & Cia
Clients Ajuntament de Manresa
Ajuntament de Vic Cambra Oficial de
Comerç i Indústria de Manresa
Cambra oficial de Comerç Indústria i
Navegació de Barcelona Caixa de
Manresa Caixa de Manlleu
Creative Director Marc Ros
Art Director David Espluga
Photographer Rafael Vargas
Collaborators Xavi Gassol Laura Armet
Copywriter Marc Ros
Graphic Designer David Espluga

2   Print Advertising
Magazine Advertising

National Award Gold
Title Airbag, Camel
Agency Tandem Campmany Guasch
DDB, SA
Client Audi
Creative Director J L Rois
Art Director Dani Ilario
Copywriter Alberto Astorga
Photographer Ricardo Miras
Retouch/Finish Grafi Image

Four airbags in the Audi range.
Average consumption 6.81 every
100km. 150HP. 222km/h.
From 0 to 100 in 8.9 seconds. New
Audi A4 TDI V6.

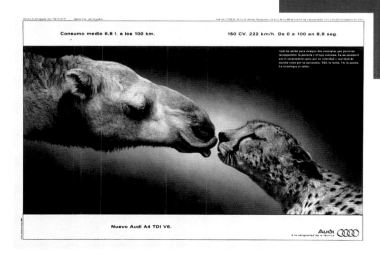

3 Print Advertising
Public Service/Charity

National Award Gold
Title A Bruit Secret
Design Studio Eumo Gràfic
Client Ajuntament de Vic
Art Director Jordi Cano
Designers Albert Cano
Anton Granero

Posters for exhibitions of contemporary
art in churches at the city of Vic.

4 TV & Cinema Advertising
Television Commercial

National Award Silver
Title Babies
Agency FCB/Tapsa
Client Siemens
Creative Director Julián Zuazo
Art Director Yuri Alemany
Copywriter Oriol Villar
Agency Producer Jesus Becedas
Film Director Paul Arden
Production Company Tesauro
Music Sintonía 1

Frank proves that his S-19 eliminates
background noise. In this case the
noise is 30 babies howling.

7 TV & Cinema Advertising
Television Commercial

National Award Silver
Title Traffic
Agency FCB/Tapsa
Client Siemens
Creative Director Julián Zuazo
Art Director Yuri Alemany
Copywriter Oriol Villar
Agency Producer Jesús Becedas
Film Director Paul Arden
Production Company Tesauro
Music Sintonía 1

Frank proves that his S-10 eliminates
background noise, even in a traffic jam
with 50 cars blasting their horns.

8 TV & Cinema Advertising
Television Commercial

National Award Gold
Title Rebuilding
Agency Tiempo/BBDO
Client Gran Teatre del Liceu
Creative Director Siscu Molina
Art Director Jordi Comas
Copywriter Eva Conesa
Designer Jordi Comas
Agency Producer Anna Morell
Film Director Pedro Aznar
Production Company Shot By
Pedro Aznar
Music Tchaikovsky

The work to rebuild the "Gran Teatre
del liceu" – Barcelona's Opera House –
is now in full swing. This is shown
here through words which describe the
special moment the liceu is
experiencing: art, inspiration, history
and, of course, opera.

Prueba número diez. ¿Me oyes bien?

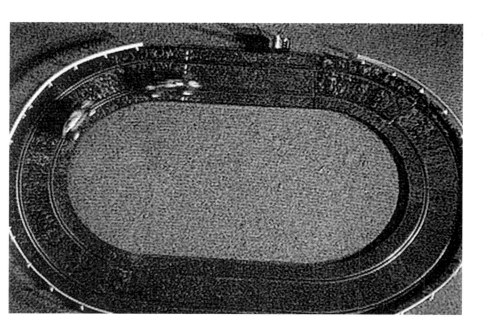

9   TV & Cinema Advertising
    Television Commercial

    National Award Gold
    Title Scalextric
    Agency BDDP/Mancebo-Kaye
    Client + Música
    Creative Directors Jorge López
    Pablo Monzón
    Art Director Jorge López
    Agency Producer Ana Pérez-Cela
    Film Director Jorge del Rey
    Production Company + Música
    Copywriter Pablo Monzón

¿LE PARECE
BIEN EN
MEDIO
AMBIENTE?

10 TV & Cinema Advertising
    Television Commercial

    National Award Silver
    Title Stars
    Agency FCB/Tapsa
    Client Caja Madrid
    Creative Director Julián Zuazo
    Art Director Julián Zuazo
    Copywriter José Carnero
    Agency Producer Jesús Becedas
    Film Director Bruce StClair
    Production Company Lee Films
    Music Eduardo Molinero

    At Caja Madrid they look after
    protecting the environment so that
    memories don't just live on in our
    imagination.

Segovia, siglo I d.C.

11 TV & Cinema Advertising
Television Commercial

National Award Gold
Title Romans
Agency FCB/Tapsa
Client Caja Madrid
Creative Director Julián Zuazo
Art Director Julián Zuazo
Copywriter José Carnero
Agency Producer Jesús Becedas
Film Director Bruce Stclair
Production Company Lee Films
Music Eduardo Molinero

At Caja Madrid they make sure that
National Heritage monuments stay
standing, even the ones that were built
nearly 2000 years ago.

12 TV & Cinema Advertising
Television Commercial

National Award Silver
Title Museum
Agency FCB/Tapsa
Client Siemens
Creative Director Julián Zuazo
Art Director Yuri Alemany
Copywriter Oriol Villar
Agency Producer Jesús Becedas
Film Director Paul Arden
Production Company Tesauro
Music Sintonía 1

Frank proves that his S-10 doesn't pick
up background noises. He speaks from
a room in a museum where the alarm
has "accidentally" been set off.

¿Escuchas algún ruido de fondo?

13 TV & Cinema Advertising
Television Commercial

National Award Gold
Title Baseball bat
Agency BDDP/Mancebo-Kaye
Client + Música
Creative Directors Jorge López
Pablo Monzón
Art Director Jorge López
Copywriter Pablo Monzón
Agency Producer Ana Pérez-Cela
Film Director Jorge del Rey
Production Company + Música
Music Frank Zappen

14 TV & Cinema Advertising
Television Commercial

National Award Gold
Title Desert
Agency BDDP/Mancebo-Kaye
Client + Musica
Creative Directors Jorge López
Pablo Monzón
Art Director Jorge López
Copywriter Pablo Monzón
Agency Producer Ana Pérez-Cela
Film Director Jorge del Rey
Production Company + Música
Music Frank Zappen

15 TV & Cinema Advertising
Television Commercial

National Award Silver
Title Bicycle
Agency Delvico Bates Barcelona SA
Client Esencial Mediterráneo
Creative Directors Julio Wallovits
Elvio Sánchez
Art Director Antonio Gómez
Copywriter Isabel Lopez
Agency Producer Pespuntes
Film Director Antonio Gómez

16 TV & Cinema Advertising
Television Commercial

National Award Silver
Title Animals
Agency Tandem Campmany
Guasch DDB SA
Client S A Damm
Creative Director J L Rois
Art Director Jürgen T Krieger
Agency Producer Pedro Ramírez
Film Director Tom Savin
Production Company Monkey Films

17 TV & Cinema Advertising
Television Commercial

National Award Gold
Title Casserole
Agency BDDP/Mancebo-Kaye
Client + Música
Creative Directors Jorge López
Pablo Monzón
Art Director Jorge López
Copywriter Pablo Monzón
Agency Producer Ana Pérez-Cela
Film Director Jorge del Rey
Production Company + Música
Music Frank Zappen

18 TV & Cinema Advertising
Television Commercial

National Award Gold
Title Energy
Agency Grey Trace
Client Panrico - Bollycao
Creative Directors Jaume Solé
Angel Trallero
Art Director Nuria Macià
Copywriter Enric Baeza
Film Director Sergi Capellas
Director of Photography Miquel Rosselló
Production Company Errecerre
Music Only you

Bollycao. There is no limit for you.

19 TV & Cinema Advertising
Television Commercial

National Award Gold
Title Price
Agency FCB/Tapsa
Client Air Europa
Creative Director Julián Zuazo
Art Director Julián Zuazo
Copywriter Enrique Pigni
Agency Producers Jesús Becedas
Fernando Garciá-Ruiz
Film Director Arnaldo
Production Company Videophot

At Air Europa our aircraft fleet is so
modern that they've even forgotten to
take the price off.

20 TV & Cinema Advertising
Television Commercial

National Award Silver
Title Beach
Agency Tiempo/BBDO
Client Centre Òptic Del Vallés
Creative Director Siscu Molina
Art Director Gabriel Penalva
Copywriter Siscu Molina
Designer Gabriel Penalva
Agency Producer Rosa M Díaz
Film Director Albert Cruells
Production Company
Albert Cruells Films
Music La Clua

If you have problems with your
eyesight, a peaceful day on the beach
could turn into a nightmare. That's
why the Opticians Centre Òptic Del
Vallés is offering prescription graduated
sunglasses at a very special price.

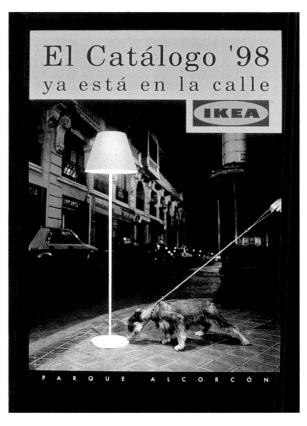

21 Posters
Poster Advertising

National Award Silver
Title New Catalogue
Agency Delvico Bates SA
Client Ikea España, AB
Creative Directors Pedro Soler
Enrique Astuy Delfín Martín
Art Director Jorge Amich
Copywriter Juan Carlos Salas
Photographer David Levin

The '98 collection has hit the streets.

22 Posters
Poster Advertising

National Award Gold
Title Naked
Agency TV Dabo
Client Andreas Claus/Lluis Llach
Art Director Joan Sibina
Designer Lidia Carrasco
Producer Andreas Claus
Banderoles Marc Martí/Signes

The aim is to communicate the message
of Lluís Llachś performance: "Nu",
which means the singer alone and just
with an instrument on the stage.

23 Promotion

National Award Silver
Title A Thousand Acres, Twin Town
Photographing Fairies, Trainspotting
Agency Barro - Testa
Client Polygram Films España
Creative Team Barro - Testa
The jury awarded the Trainspotting
Press book a nomination

26 Graphic Design
Corporate Identity

National Award Gold
Title Booket
Design Studio Summa
Comunicació, SA
Client Ediciones De Bolsillo
Creative Directors Xavier Bas
Josep Maria Mir Claret Serrahima
Copywriter Xavier Grau
Designer Sean Bolan

Name and corporate identity for a new
brand in pocket books belonging to the
largest publishing group in Spain.

27 Graphic Design
Corporate Identity

National Award Silver
Title Demostra
Design Studio CM &C Disseny
Client Ajuntament de Sant
Sadurní d' Anoia
Designers Esther Carbó
Jordi March Paula Canals

Demostra "Prove it", with many
senses.
Mostra Exhibition.
Most Must. Sant Sadurní is the centre
of the Penedès wine region.
Osta Expression of surprise and
admiration and art.

28 Graphic Design
TV Graphics

National Award Gold
Title BTV TV Graphics
Designer Peret
Client Institut de Comunicació de Barcelona
Creative Director Peret
Graphic Designers Peret
Mariola Mariño Mariona Omedes
Film Director Marina Omedes
Production Company BTV
Music X. Capelles R Martínez

29 Packaging

National Award Gold
Title CHCL Packaging
Design Studio Munt Barcelona
Client CHCL Duch Claramunt Joiers
Creative Director Xavier Claramunt
Art Director Miquel de Mas
Designers Xavier Claramunt
Miquel de Mas
Photographer Giovanni Zanzi
Illustrators Elena Batet Pep Valls

Packs for a contemporary design company, thought to "open and find", through unfolding and searching.

30 Packaging

National Award Silver
Title Ishtar Cosmetics Packaging
Design Studio Nacho Lavernia y Asociados, S.L.
Client Ishtar Cosmetic SL
Designers Nacho Lavernia
Alberto Cienfuegos
Photographer Enric Pérez

Design of packaging for a line of cosmetics.

31 Editorial

National Award Silver
Title Youth Diary 1998
Design Studio Estudio Lanzagorta
Client Ayuntamiento de Donostia-San Sebastián
Art Director José Luis Lanzagorta
Designer José Luis Lanzagorta

Youth diary in favour of human rights.

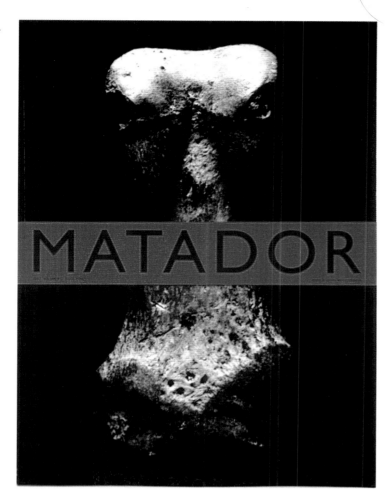

32 Editorial

National Award Gold
Title Matador Volume C
Design Studio Grafica
Client La Fabrica
Creative Director Fernando Gutiérrez
Art Director Fernando Gutiérrez
Designers Maria Ulecia
Emanuelle Ponty

An annual magazine about the arts,
trends and ideas. A magazine that
brings people's passions together from
around the world. Volume C is based
on inventing a new name for Spain. A
geographical reference, not political.

33 Editorial

National Award Silver
Title The Commercials Book
Design Studio Grafica
Client D&AD
Creative Director Mike Dempsey
Art Director Fernando Gutiérrez
Designers Fernando Gutiérrez
Emanuelle Ponty
Photographer Oliviero Toscani

NÄMEN!
ÄR DET INTE
JAPANS
FLAGGA SOM
HÄNGER DÄR!

BÄTTRE LOKALSINNE **GP**

Sweden

1 **Gold**
Posters
Poster Advertising

National Award Silver
Title Local knowledge
Agency Forsman & Bodenfors
Client Göteborgs-Posten
Art Director Staffan Forsman
Copywriter Björn Engström

This campaign for Göteborg-Posten
emphasises its local knowledge, as
every poster comments on something in
very close proximity of the poster site.

This is an example of the campaign
that covered over 50% of the outdoor
objects in Göteborg.

Göteborgs-Posten is the second largest
morning paper in Sweden.

2 Nomination
Print Advertising
Magazine Advertising

National Award Silver
Title Diesel Historical Moments
Agency Paradiset DDB
Client Diesel
Creative Director Joakim Jonason
Art Director Joakim Jonason
Copywriter Jacob Nelson
Photographer Peter Gehrke
Account Director Stefan Öström
Account Manager Mia Kleist

3 Nomination
TV & Cinema Advertising
Television Commercial

National Award Silver
Title Internet
Agency Garbergs Annonsbyrå
Client Telenordia Internet
Art Director Petter Ödeen
Copywriter Johan van der Schoot
Agency Producer Marie Arvidsson
Film Director Axel Laubscher
Director of Photography Philip Ögaard
Production Company Mekano
Film & Television

A young woman is getting dressed. She is constantly ringing her friend excitedly. She tells her friend she's met someone on the internet.
She downloads his homepage to get a look at him, the downloading goes extremely slowly.
Finally, half the homepage reveals a man with 'movie star' good looks. Now she's really excited.
She hasn't time to see the whole homepage, because she has to leave for her date.
Just after she's left, we see the rest of the homepage.
We see that the goodlooking man is actually a poster on the wall. Below the poster, sitting on the sofa is a very overweight, not so good looking man. He burps continuously on his homepage.
Super: Choose a faster internet.

 4

 5

4   **Nomination**
TV & Cinema Advertising
Television Commercial

National Award Gold
Title Little Rock, 1873
Agency Paradiset DDB
Client Diesel
Creative Director Joakim Jonason
Art Director Joakim Jonason
Copywriter Jacob Nelson
Agency Producers Stefan Öström
Mia Kleist
Production Company Traktor

It's high noon in Little Rock. It's the
worst of them all versus Mr Handsome
in a pair of Diesel jeans with a perfect
fit. It's showdown time.
Diesel. For successful living.

5   **Nomination**
TV & Cinema Advertising
Television Commercial

National Award Silver
Title The teacher
Agency Forsman & Bodenfors
Client Volvo PB Sverige
Copywriters Oscar Askelöf
Filip Nilsson
Agency Producer Maria Bergkvist
Director of Photography
Tim Maurice Jones
Production Company Traktor

6 Nomination
   Graphic Design
   Corporate Identity

National Award Silver
Title Rabiega
Agency OCH-Herrmann,
Liljendahl & Co AB
Client Vin & Sprit AB
Creative Director Greger Ulf Nilson
Art Director Greger Ulf Nilson
Designers Greger Ulf Nilson
Igor Kazakoff

7 **Print Advertising**
Newspaper Advertising

National Award Silver
Title Snow
Agency Forsman & Bodenfors
Client Volvo PB Sverige
Art Director Anders Eklind
Copywriter Filip Nilsson

The Volvo V70 All-Wheel Drive.

8 **Print Advertising**
Newspaper Advertising

National Award Silver
Title Be first in Djursholm
Agency Rönnberg McCann
Client Wetterling
Art Director Catt Olsson
Copywriter Carl Lewenhaupt
Illustrator Jane Hammond

9   Print Advertising
    Newspaper Advertising

National Award Silver
Title Nordiska campaign
Agency Romson
Client Nordiska Kompaniet
Art Director Anna Romson
Copywriter Ola Gatby
Photographers Carl Bengtsson
Lasse Kärkinen

Not since Adam and Eve were
scrumping apples has fashion felt as
natural as this spring. The colour range
is the same as our skin. The silhouette
matches our bodies. The shape follows
the body, transparent and supple.
Welcome to a spring of fundamental
fashion at Nordiska Kompaniet. Why
not start by visiting Donna Karan's
DKNY spring première on Floor 1.

10 Print Advertising
    Trade Advertising

National Award Gold
Title Swedish Provinces
Agency Ahlqvist & Co
Client Nordsjö AB
Creative Director Christer Strandberg
Art Director Christer Strandberg
Photographers Hans Hammarskiöld
Sune Jonsson Gerry Johansson
Pål-Nils Nilsson Peder Björkegrenl

11 **Print Advertising**
Public Service/Charity

National Award Silver
Title Schizophrenia campaign
Agency Lundberg & Co
Client Riks IFS Swedish
Schizophrenia Fellowship
Creative Director Tommy Lundberg
Art Director Maria Källberg-Johansson
Copywriter Tommy Lundberg
Illustrator Bengt Anderung

We want to give schizophrenia one
identity.

12 **TV & Cinema Advertising**
Television Commercial

National Award Silver
Title Trainee
Agency Stenström & Co
Client AB Svenska Smör
Art Director Bertil Åström
Copywriter Anders Lidzell
Film Director Olavi Häkkinen
Director of Photography Jens Fischer
Production Company Oh-La-La

Trainee at the butter factory.

13 TV & Cinema Advertising
Television Commercial

National Award Silver
Title A day in P'yongyang
Agency Paradiset DDB
Client Diesel
Creative Director Joakim Jonason
Art Director Joakim Jonason
Copywriter Jacob Nelson
Agency Producers Stefan Öström
Mia Kleist
Production Company Traktor

The story about a young man in North Korea and a day in his life where he fights with his father, dresses in jeans, picks up his girlfriend, rides his bike to the bus-station, takes the bus to the city, is refused into the community hall because of the way he is dressed, looses his girlfriend and hits for the bridge where he thinks about leaving it all behind.
Diesel.
For successful living.

14 TV & Cinema Advertising
Television Commercial

National Award Silver
Title The golfer
Agency Forsman & Bodenfors
Client Volvo PB Sverige
Copywriters Filip Nilsson
Oscar Askelöf
Agency Producer Maria Bergkvist
Production Company Traktor
Director of Photography
Tim Maurice Jones

The two dots symbolize the two holes
in a Swedish wall socket.

17 **Posters**
Poster Advertising

National Award Silver
Title Image campaign spring 97
Agency OCH–Herrmann,
Liljendahl & Co AB
Client Vattenfall AB
Creative Director Lars Liljendahl
Art Director Lars Liljendahl
Copywriter Mattias Jersild
Designer Kerstin Bernander
Illustrator John Jacobsson

The two dots symbolize the two
holes in a Swedish wall socket.

18 **Posters**
Poster Advertising

National Award Silver
Title 90 kilometres of fashion
Agency Romson
Client Nordiska Kompaniet
Art Directors Anna Romson
Magnus Ingerstedt
Copywriter Ola Gatby
Photographers Bruce Weber
Ellen von Umwerth Mapple Thorpe

-Nu måste jag vattna blommorna igen. Häng kvar.

E2.TELE2.TEL.
DU RINGER LÅNGT BILLIGARE MED 007.

RING SÅ SPRÄNGER JAG! DU HITTAR MIN LILLA ANNONS I GP VARJE DAG.

19 Posters
Poster Advertising

National Award Silver
Title Tele2 campaign
Agency Paradiset DDB
Client Tele2
Creative Director Joakim Jonason
Art Director Joakim Jonason
Copywriter Jens Englund

I have to water my flowers again.
Hold on.

20 Posters
Poster Advertising

National Award Silver
Title Classifieds
Agency Forsman & Bodenfors
Client Göteborgs-Posten
Art Directors Staffan Forsman
Henrik Delehag
Copywriters Björn Engström
Martin Ringqvist Frida Omsén

This local campaign for the classified section of Göteborg-Posten, Göteborg's largest morning paper, consists of more than 1,400 different posters.

Each poster is hand-made and unique, and refers to an actual small ad, published in GP the week of the campaign.

21 Promotion

National Award Silver
Title Welcome home
Agency OCH–Herrmann,
Liljendahl & Co AB
Client Svenska Turistföreningen
Creative Director Greger Ulf Nilson
Art Director Greger Ulf Nilson
Copywriter Claes Kjellström
Designers Greger Ulf Nilson
Judith Wernholm
Photographers Mikael Andersson
Stina Brockman Björn Dawidsson

Bruno Ehrs Nina Ericson
Thomas Fahlander Neil Goldstein
Claes Grundsten Denise Grünstein
Putte Hallberg & Son Jonas Ingerstedt
Lena Johansson Bertil Karlsson
Björn Keller Per Klaesson
Irmelie Krekin Lars Liljendahl
Bosse Lind Magnus Mårding
Ulf Huett Nilsson P-O Norman
Bengt-Olof Olsson Ulf Owenede
Ewa-Marie Rundqvist
Karl-Roland Schröter
Niclas Sjögren

22 Promotion

National Award Silver
Title Pang Pang Campaign
Agency Allansson & Nilsson
Client Pang Pang
Art Director Malin Köhlmark
Copywriter Olof Gustafsson
Photographer Mikael Olsson
Account Supervisors Charlotta
Warnhammar Ulrika Enghage
Original Anette Eskilsson
Advertisers Supervisors Pernilla
Warnhammar Helena Åkerström

Ett antal
användbara
horisontlinjer.

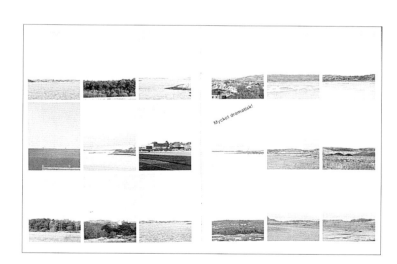

23 Promotion

National Award Silver
Title Badges & tattoos
Agency Garberg Annonsbyrå
Client MTV Networks
Art Director John Mara
Copywriters Totte Stub
Martin Gumpert
Designer John Mara
Photographer Mike Adevica/Up

24 Promotion
Mailings

National Award Silver
Title Swedish Post campaign
Agency Romson
Client Sweden Post
Art Director Magnus Ingerstedt
Copywriter Johan Olivero

Here...in this box lies 800 dollars.
Unfortunately we couldn't give you the
key in the ad.

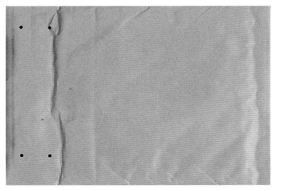

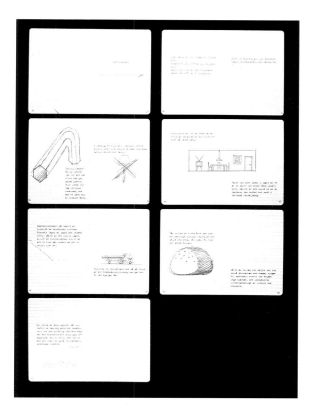

25 Promotion
Mailings

National Award Gold
Title Homework
Agency Forsman & Bodenfors
Client IKEA Svenska Försäljnings AB
Art Director Anders Eklind
Copywriter Filip Nilsson
Illustrator Anders Eklind

This booklet, designed as a Swedish
school exercise book, was given to all
IKEA employees in Sweden. It explains
the company's future strategy and how
easily each employee can contribute to
making the strategy reality.

26 Graphic Design
Corporate Identity

National Award Gold
Title King's Dog Ale/Kungsholmens
Kalasöl/Kungsholmens
Kryssaröl/Tomtefar
Agency OCH-Herrmann,
Liljendahl & Co AB
Client Kungsholmens Kvartersbryggeri
Creative Director Lars Liljendahl
Art Director Lars Liljendahl
Designer Kerstin Bernander
Illustrator Håkan Lundgren

27 Graphic Design

National Award Silver
Title Astrom, Austrøm, Āstroem,
Åström
Agency NybergDesign
Client CV Search
Art Director Kent Nyberg
Designers Kent Nyberg
Johannes Svartholm

28 Graphic Design

National Award Silver
Title Design Sigvard Bernadotte
Agency Forsman & Bodenfors
Client National Museum
Art Director Anders Kornestedt
Designer Anders Kornestedt
Copywriters Sigvard Bernadotte
Micael Ernstell and others
Photographer Per-Magnus Persson &
various private picture sources

Hakle Toilettenpapier. Für absolute Sauberkeit.

1   Gold
    Print Advertising
    Newspaper Advertising

    National Award Gold
    Title Hakle Spalt
    Agency Advico Young & Rubicam
    Client Hakle AG
    Creative Director Martin Spillmann
    Art Directors Martin Spillmann
    Roland Scotoni
    Copywriters Martin Spillmann
    Urs Schrepfer

3

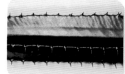

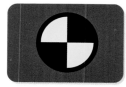

smart
reduce to the max.

http://www.smart.com
hotline 0801 803 803, 0,90 F/min.

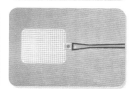

4

STOPPT DEN ANTISEMITISMUS IN DER SCHWEIZ, BEVOR ES ZU SPÄT IST.

3 Nomination
Promotion
Mailings

National Award Silver
Title Smart: rttm cards
Agency Weber, Hodel, Schmid,
Client Micro Compact Car AG
Creative Director Liliane Lerch
Art Directors Juerg Aemmer
Thomas Von Ah
Copywriter Liliane Lerch
Photographers Alf Dietrich
Katrin Freisager Stefan Minder
Scheffold Vizner Stefan Indlekofer
Thomas Eugster Anatol Kotte
Art Buying Nicole Suter

4 Nomination
Posters
Public Service/Charity

National Award Silver
Title Stop anti-semitism
Agency McCann-Erickson
Client Aktionskomitee gegen
Antisemitismus in der Schweiz
Creative Director Edi Andrist
Art Directors Martin Bettler
Ernst Bächtold
Copywriter Claude Catsky

5 **Nomination**
Illustration & Photography
Photography

National Award Gold
Title The Smart Book
Agency Weber, Hodel, Schmid,
Client Micro Compact Car AG
Creative Directors Beda Achermann
Peter Ruch
Art Directors Markus Bucher
Ercole Troisi Juerg Aemmer

Copywriter Peter Ruch
Photographers Martin Parr
François Caraco Daniel Sutter
Nitin Vadukul Urs Moeckli
Hans Gissinger Raymond Meier
Max Vadukul Thomas Flechtner
François Halard Michel Comte
Glen Luchford Patricia von Ah
Illustrators Sandro Fabbri
Jean-Phillippe Delhomme
Mats Gustafson Maurice Vellekoop
Monic Baumann

6 **Nomination**
Illustration & Photography
Illustration

National Award Silver
Title ADC Jahrbuch 1997
Agency Advico Young & Rubicam
Client ADC CH
Art Director Roland Scotoni
Illustrator Brad Holland

Fotos: Raymond Meier
Trauen Sie Ihren Augen nicht. Alles, was Sie sehen, kann auch ganz anders
sein. Sogar die Farben des smart: Rot, Gelb, Schwarz, Weiß. Denn Farbensehen
ist so kompliziert, daß noch nicht einmal die Forscher durchblicken.

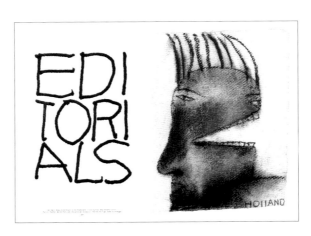

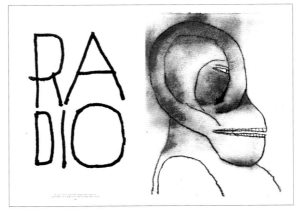

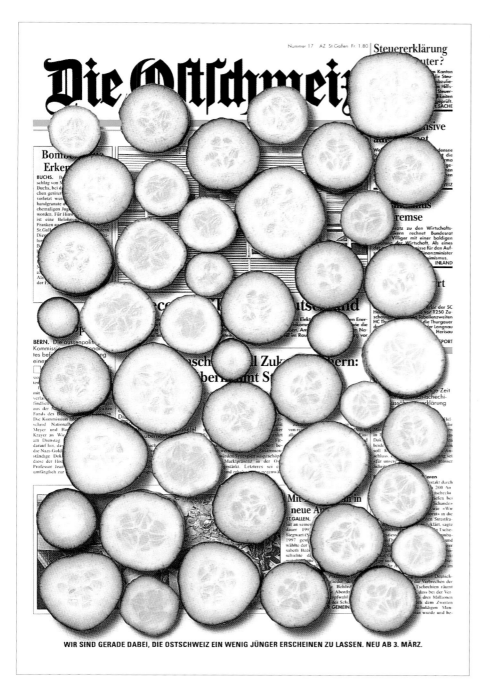

WIR SIND GERADE DABEI, DIE OSTSCHWEIZ EIN WENIG JÜNGER ERSCHEINEN ZU LASSEN. NEU AB 3. MÄRZ.

7   Print Advertising
Newspaper Advertising

National Award Silver
Title Redesign Ostschweiz
Agency Wirz Werbeberatung AG
Client Die Ostschweiz
Creative Director André Benker
Art Director Mario Ferrara
Copywriter Daniel Müller
Photographer Markus Weber

8   Print Advertising
Newspaper Advertising

National Award Silver
Title Hakle recipes
Agency Advico Young & Rubicam
Client Hakle AG
Creative Director Martin Spillmann
Art Directors Martin Spillmann
Roland Scotoni
Copywriters Martin Spillmann
Urs Schrepfer

9 **Print Advertising**
   Newspaper Advertising

   National Award Silver
   Title Publicitas
   Agency Publicis, Farner, Aebi, Strebel
   Client Publicitas SA
   Creative Director Jean Etienne Aebi
   Art Director René Sennhauser
   Copywriter Beat Reck
   Illustrator Michael Sowa

10 **Print Advertising**
   Newspaper Advertising

   National Award Gold
   Title Post robbery
   Agency Advico Young & Rubicam
   Client Mazda (Switzerland)
   Creative Director Martin Spillmann
   Art Director Denis Schwarz
   Copywriters Urs Schrepfer
   Peter Brönnimann
   Photographer Peter Forster

   The Mazda E 2000 would have had
   space for even 70 million francs.

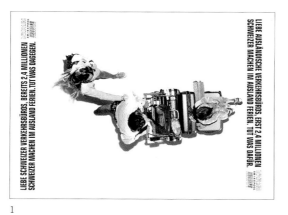

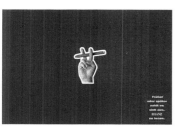

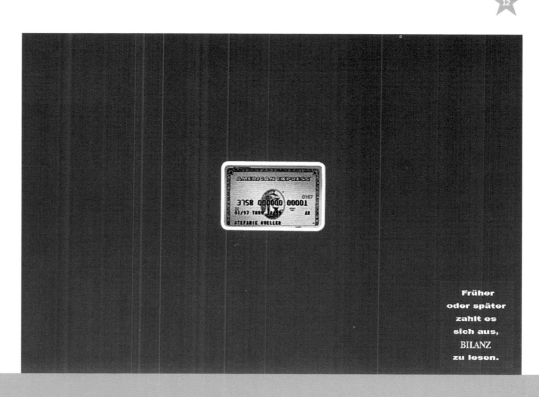

11 Print Advertising
Newspaper Advertising

National Award Silver
Title Swisspool
Agency Publicis, Farner, Aebi, Strebel
Client Swisspool
Creative Director Jean Etienne Aebi
Art Director Jürg Aemmer
Copywriter Matthias Freuler
Photographer Anatol Kotte

1. Notice to foreign tourist offices: Only 1.4 miilion Swiss spend their holidays abroad. Do something for it.

Notice to Swiss tourist offices: Already 1.4 million Swiss spend their holidays abroad. Do something against it.
2. Notice to department stores: Only 15% of all clothes are sold in our branches. Do something for it.
Notice to fashion dealers: Already 15% of all clothes are sold at department stores. Do something against it.
3. Notice to foreign brewers: Only 600,000 hl of beer are imported to Switzerland. Do something for it.
Notice to Swiss brewers: Already 600,000 hl of beer are imported from abroad. Do something against it.

12 Print Advertising
Newspaper Advertising

National Award Silver
Title Bilanz
Agency Publicis, Farner, Aebi, Strebel
Client Bilanz
Creative Director Claude Martin
Art Director Luigi Del Medico
Copywriters Thomas Kurzmeyer
Claude Catsky
Photographer Patrick Rohner

13 Print Advertising
  Magazine Advertising

National Award Silver
Title Facts
Agency Publicis, Farner, Aebi, Strebel
Client Facts Publishing House
Creative Director Jean Etienne Aebi
Art Director Erik Voser
Copywriter Matthias Freuler
Photographer Chris Frazer Smith

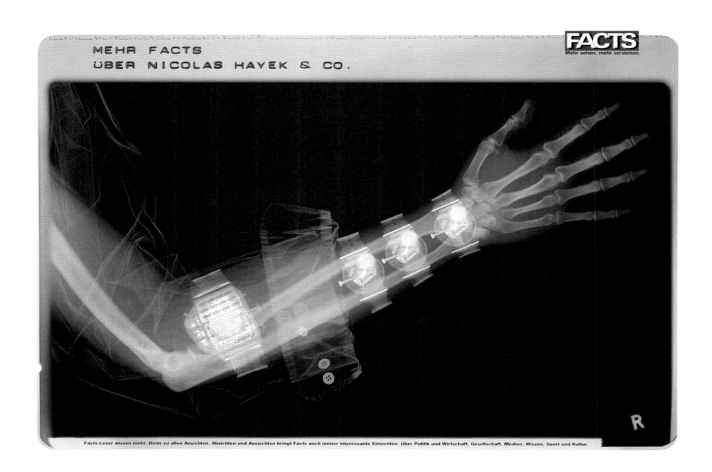

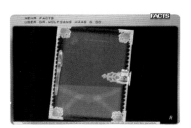

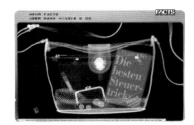

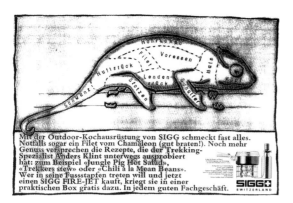

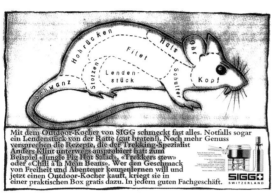

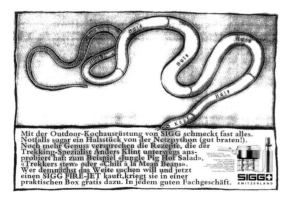

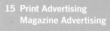

14 Print Advertising
Magazine Advertising

National Award Silver
Title Sigg outdoor survive ads
Agency Publicis, Farner, Aebi, Strebel
Client Sigg
Creative Director Claude Martin
Art Director Luigi Del Medico
Copywriter Markus Ruf
Photographer PICT
Illustrators Markus Wyss
Marcel Fässler

15 Print Advertising
Magazine Advertising

National Award Silver
Title SF 2
Agency Advico Young & Rubicam
Client Swiss TV
Creative Director Hansjörg Zürcher
Art Director Dana Wirz
Copywriter Urs Schrepfer
Photographer Julien Vonier

16

16 Print Advertising
Trade Advertising

National Award Gold
Title RTL 2
Agency Guye & Partner
Client IP Multimedia
Art Director Patrick Rychner
Copywriter Markus Ruf
Photographer Urs Dürst

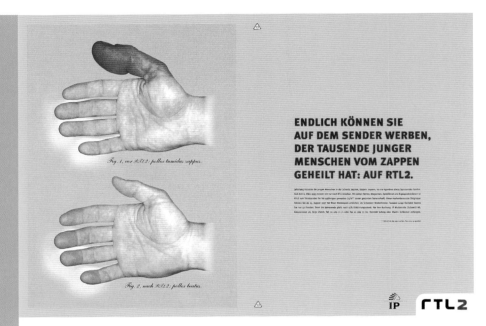

Fig. 1, vor RTL2: pollex tumidus zappus.

Fig. 2, nach RTL2: pollex beatus.

ENDLICH KÖNNEN SIE
AUF DEM SENDER WERBEN,
DER TAUSENDE JUNGER
MENSCHEN VOM ZAPPEN
GEHEILT HAT: AUF RTL2.

17 Print Advertising
Trade Advertising

National Award Silver
Title Job-offer ad
Agency Weber, Hodel, Schmid,
Client Weber, Hodel, Schmid,
Creative Director Reinhold Weber
Art Director Simone Fennel
Copywriter Beat Egger

Well known copywriters' and
Account Directors' names are
(incorrectly) proof-read. General
idea: improve your skills in
advertising with Weber, Hodel,
Schmid.

Claude Catsky, Andreas Prokesch,
Johannes Jost, Harry Sulzer,
Markus Ruf, Mike Krüll, Martin Suter,
André Benker, Robert Stalder,
Frank Baumann, Matthias Freuler,
Dr. Joni Müller, Patrick Schräg,
David Honegger, Jean-Etienne Aebi,

Konstantin Jacoby, Wolfgang Sasse,
Dörte Spengler, Oliver Voss,
Sebastian Turner, Gerald Heinemann,
Werner Knopf, André Aimaq,
Patrick Schräg, Detmar Karpinski,
Olaf Oldigs, Mirko Vasata,
Carsten Heintzsch, André Kemper,

Patricia Meneghin, Fredy Weisser,
Manfred Hager, Ursula Krebs,
Kurt Schmid, Achim Wirtz, Elke Zappe,
Barbara Weber, Michel Benker,
Christophe Guye, Reto Alborghetti,
Tobias Trevisan, Cornelia Harder,
Susanne Dürrenmatt, Andy Hostettler,

18 Print Advertising
Trade Advertising

National Award Silver
Title Facts
Agency Publicis, Farner, Aebi, Strebel
Client Facts Publishing House
Creative Director Jean Etienne Aebi
Art Director Jürg Aemmer
Copywriter Matthias Freuler

19 Print Advertising
Trade Advertising

National Award Silver
Title Nico image campaign
Agency McCann-Erickson
Client TA Media AG
Creative Director Edi Andrist
Art Director Nicolas Vontobel
Copywriter Claude Catsky

20 Print Advertising
Public Service / Charity

National Award Gold
Title Anti-racism campaign
Agency Impuls. BDDP
Client Swiss Federal Commission
Against Racism
Creative Director Felix Zimmermann
Art Director Oliver Schneider
Copywriter Frank W Bienenfeld
Photographer Alberto Venzago

1. Kofi Zuberbühler, 8: "The Swiss like
me a lot. As long as I'm small and cute."
2. Lee Hua, 30, cook: "I'm welcome
here. As long as my food tastes good."
3. Enver and Albana, Refugees: "The
neighbours accept us. As long as we
don't leave the compound."
4. Tee Cee Cole, 33, DJ: "I'm part of
the action. As long as I stay put at the
turntable."

21 Print Advertising
Public Service / Charity

National Award Silver
Title Drive clean
Agency McCann-Erickson
Client Vereinigung für Familien der
Strassenopfer (VFS)
Creative Director Frank Bodin
Art Director Urs Hartmann
Copywriter Stefan Gigon
Photographer Urs Maurer

1 2 3 4

Enver und Albana, Asylsuchende: «Die Nachbarn dulden uns.

Enver und Albana, Asylsuchende: «Die Nachbarn dulden uns.

Gedankenlosigkeit führt in der Schweiz jedes Jahr zu Tausenden von Bränden.

BfB. Beratungsstelle für Brandverhütung.

Solang' wir die Unterkunft nicht verlassen.»

22 TV & Cinema Advertising
Public Service/Charity

National Award Silver
Title Randolph
Agency Advico Young & Rubicam
Client Advisory Board to Prevent
Fire Damage
Creative Director Martin Spillmann
Art Director Sacha Moser
Copywriter Rudolph Schürmann
Film Directors Martin Fueter
Detlef Henrichs
Production Company Condor Films,
Zürich

23 TV & Cinema Advertising
Public Service/Charity

National Award Gold
Title Anti-racism campaign
Agency Impuls. BDDP
Client Swiss Federal Commission
against Racism
Creative Director Felix Zimmermann
Art Director Oliver Schneider
Copywriter Frank W. Bienenfeld
Film Director Alberto Venzago
Director of Photography
Alberto Venzago

24 TV & Cinema Advertising
Cinema Commercial

National Award Silver
Title UBS poems
Agency Advico Young & Rubicam
Client UBS/Union Bank of Switzerland
Creative Director Martin Spillmann
Agency Producer Michela Trümpi
Film Director Neil French
Production Company Union
Commercial London

25 TV & Cinema Advertising
Cinema Commercial

National Award Silver
Title Swisscom
Agency Wirz Werbeberatung AG
Client Swisscom COM-US
Creative Director André Benker
Art Director Jörg Birker
Copywriter Hanspeter Schweizer
Agency Producer Lilo Killer
Film Director Thomas Krygier
Director of Photography
Damian Morisot
Production Company
Arden Sutherland-Dodd

26 TV & Cinema Advertising
Television Commercial

National Award Silver
Title The power of Panasonic
Agency Honegger/von Matt
Client John Lay Electronics
Creative Director David Honegger
Art Directors Dany Bieri
Susan Gehrig
Copywriter Claudia Kohler-Fehringer
Film Director Ernst Wirz
Director of Photography
Thomas Albrecht
Production Company Wirz & Fraefel

27 TV & Cinema Advertising
Television Commercial

National Award Silver
Title Leather
Agency Advico Young & Rubicam
Client Swissair
Creative Director Martin Spillmann
Art Directors Paul Meijer
Martin Spillmann Silvia Rollino
Copywriters Silvia Rollino
Martin Spilmann Paul Meijer
Film Director Paul Meijer
Production Company
Planete Spots, Paris

28 TV & Cinema Advertising
Television Commercial

National Award Silver
Title Swisscom
Agency Wirz Werbeberatung AG
Client Swisscom COM-US
Creative Director André Benker
Art Director Jörg Birker
Copywriter Hanspeter Schweizer
Agency Producer Lilo Killer
Film Director Thomas Krygier
Director of Photography
Damian Morisot
Production Company
Arden Sutherland-Dodd

29 Posters
Poster Advertising

National Award Silver
Title Swisscom Berne
Agency Wirz Werbeberatung AG
Client Swisscom COM-US
Creative Director André Benker
Art Director Valentina Hermann
Copywriter Hanspeter Schweizer
Photographer Grund & Flum, Zurich

30 Posters
Poster Advertising

National Award Silver
Title Box-Champ
Agency Hess & Kiss
Client Stefan Angehrn
Creative Director Sarah Kiss
Art Director Roland Hess
Copywriter Tamás Kiss

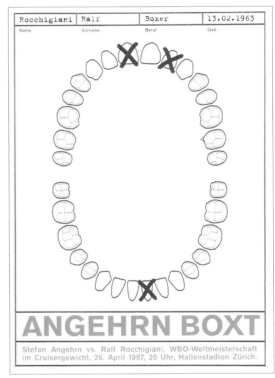

CITYBIKES.   MOUNTAINBIKES.   RACINGBIKES.

33 Posters
Poster Advertising

National Award Gold
Title Sportplausch Wider
Agency Publicis, Farner, Aebi, Strebel
Client Sportplausch Wider
Creative Directors Markus Gut
Markus Ruf
Art Director Markus Gut
Copywriter Markus Ruf
Photographer Gioni Fry

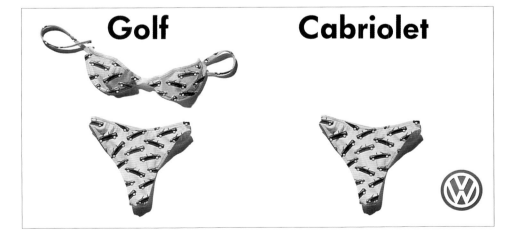

34 Posters
Poster Advertising

National Award Silver
Title Golf Cabriolet
Agency GGK Basel Werbeagentur AG
Client AMAG Import AG
Creative Director Mark Stahel
Art Director Alfred Burkard
Copywriter Lorenz Spinas
Photographer Nicolas Monkewitz

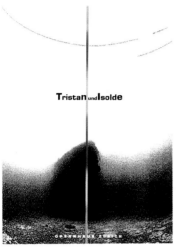

1

2

3

Tee Cee Cole, 33, DJ:
«Ich gehöre zur Partygemeinde.

Solang' ich am Plattenteller stehe.»

Enver und Albana Kodra, Asylsuchende:
«Die Nachbarn dulden uns.

Solang' wir die Unterkunft nicht verlassen.»

Kofi Zuberbühler, 8:
«Die Schweizer haben mich gern.

Solang' ich klein und herzig bin.»

35 Posters
Public Service/Charity

National Award Silver
Title Opera in pictures
Agency K D Geissbühler
Client Opernhaus Zürich
Designer K D Geissbühler

36 Posters
Public Service/Charity

National Award Gold
Title Anti-racism campaign
Agency Impuls. BDDP
Client Swiss Federal Commission
against Racism
Creative Director Felix Zimmermann
Art Director Oliver Schneider
Copywriter Frank W Bienenfeld
Photographer Alberto Venzago

1. Tee Cee Cole, 33, DJ: "I'm part of
the action. As long as I stay put at the
turntable."
2. Enver and Albana, Refugees: "The
neighbours accept us. As long as we
don't leave the compound."
3. Kofi Zuberbühler, 8: "The Swiss like
me a lot. As long as I'm small and cute."

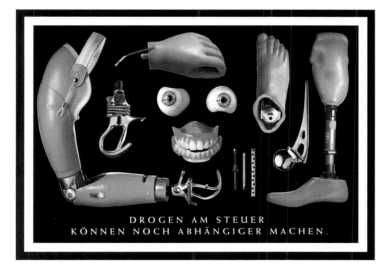

39 Promotion

National Award Silver
Title Drive clean flyer & postcard
Agency McCann-Erickson
Client Vereinigung für Familien der
Strassenopfer (VFS)
Creative Director Frank Bodin
Art Director Urs Hartmann
Copywriter Stefan Gigon
Photographer Urs Maurer

**40 Promotion
Mailings**

National Award Silver
Title Christmas card
Agency Advico Young & Rubicam
Client Advico Young & Rubicam
Creative Director Martin Spillmann
Art Director Denis Schwarz
Copywriters Urs Schrepfer
Peter Brönnimann

**41 Promotion
Mailings**

National Award Silver
Title Ecce Chlausus corporate design
manual
Design Studio Face to Face Visual and
Corporate Culture
Client Face to Face
Creative Director Mirjam Pierig
Art Director Mirjam Pierig
Copywriter Irene Seeholzer
Illustrator Mirjam Pierig

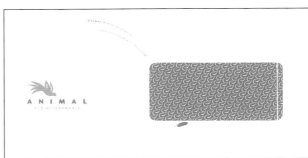

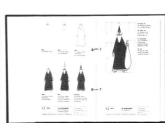

44 Graphic Design
Corporate Identity

National Award Silver
Title PTA Annual Report 1996
Agency Wirz Identity AG
Client Post Telekom Austria AG
Creative Director Urs Glaser
Art Directors Raphael Baumann
Walter Bohatsch
Designers Walter Kern
Walter Bohatsch
Photographer Markus Roessle

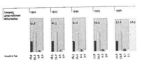

Grand Prix
TV & Cinema Advertising
Television Commercial

National Award Silver
Title The Lamp Post, Hiccups, Chair, Dentist.
Agency BMP DDB
Client Volkswagen Group
Creative Director Jeremy Craigen
Art Director Andrew Fraser
Copywriter Andrew Fraser
Agency Producer Howard Spivey
Production Company Outsider

Lamp Post
We see two men at work in a residential street. One is wrapping padding around a lamp post, and the other is putting up a poster. When the men have finished, they drive off in their van. As the van pulls away, we see that the poster says, 'Polo, only £8,145'.
After they have gone, a man in a suit walks into frame, and turns to look at the poster. He carries on walking and staring at the poster, unaware that he is about to bump into the lamp post. We now realise what the padding is for.

Hiccups
A woman is sitting at her kitchen table reading a newspaper. She is suffering from hiccups. Finally, she comes across an ad in the paper which says 'Polo, from only £7,990'. The hiccups are cured.

Chair
A woman is walking through a shopping precinct. Suddenly she feels faint, and starts to lose her balance. A passer-by comes over and helps her to a nearby bench. When, eventually, she starts to recover, she looks back along the precinct, and we see what caused the problem. There is a poster, which says 'Polo, from only £7,990'.

Dentist
A dentist tries, unsuccessfully, to persuade a patient to open his mouth wider. Finally, he tells the patient that he's just bought a Golf Gti for only £14,640. The patient's mouth drops open for him.

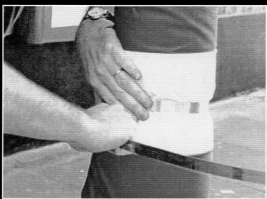

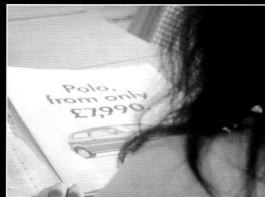

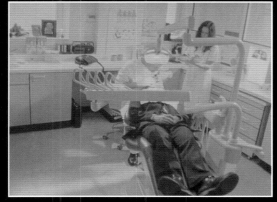

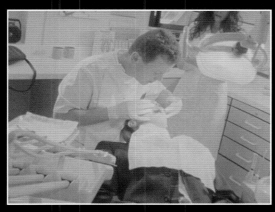

Polo,
from only
£7,990.

Surprisingly ordinary prices.

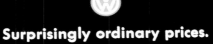

Surprisingly ordinary prices.

www.volkswagen.co.uk

www.volkswagen.co.uk

1   Gold
Print Advertising
Public Service/Charity

National Award Silver
Title Clear, Two Fingers, Cockroaches,
Draw Blood, Karen, Two Voices
Agency Saatchi & Saatchi
Client Department of Health/CO1
Creative Directors Adam Kean
Alex Taylor
Art Directors John Messum
Colin Jones
Copywriter Mike McKenna
Photographer Graham Cornthwaite
Typographer Roger Kennedy

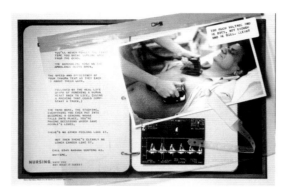

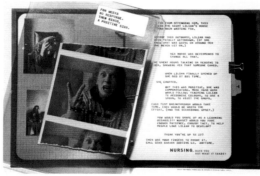

Have you ever noticed how protected you feel
when you make yourself small?

2 Gold
   TV & Cinema Advertising
   Cinema Commercial

   National Award Silver
   Title Protection
   Agency BMP DDB
   Client Volkswagen Group UK
   Creative Directors Richard Flintham
   Andy McLeod
   Art Director Jeremy Craigen
   Copywriter Jeremy Craigen
   Agency Producer Howard Spivey
   Film Director Jonathan Glazer
   Production Company
   Academy Commercials
   Lighting Camera Steve Keith-Roach

3　Gold
Illustration & Photography
Photography

National Award Silver
Title Autumn/Winter
Design Studio David James
Client Prada
Creative Director David James
Art Director David James
Photographer Glen Luchford

4 Nomination
TV & Cinema Advertising
Television Commercial

National Award Silver
Title Perfect Day
Agency Leagus Delaney
Client BBC
Creative Director Tim Delaney
Art Director Ian Ducker
Copywriter Will Farquhar
Film Director Gregory Rood
Music Composer Lou Reed
Music Director The Music Sculptors
TV Co-ordinator Julia Methold

5 Nomination
TV & Cinema Advertising
Cinema Commercial

National Award Silver
Title Parklife
Agency TBWA Simons Palmer
Client Nike UK
Creative Directors Tony Malcolm
Guy Moore
Art Director Guy Moore
Copywriter Tony Malcolm
Agency Producer Jo Sayer
Production Company
Academy Commercials

 4

5

6 **Nomination**
TV & Cinema Advertising
Cinema Commercial

National Award Silver
Title Smarienberg
Agency Lowe Howard Spink
Client The Pierre Smirnoff Company
Creative Director Paul Weinberger
Art Director Mitch Levy
Copywriter Derek Apps
Agency Producer Sue Braley
Film Director Michael Gondry
Production Company
Partizan Midi Midi

7 **Nomination**
Posters
Poster Advertising

National Award Silver
Title Eros
Agency BMP DDB
Creative Director Tony Cox
Art Director Richard Flintham
Copywriters Andy McLeod
Nick Gill Ewan Paterson
Photographer Giles Revell
Typographer Dave Wakefield

Making London simple

May 3 1997

weekend

**The world at their feet
Kathy Acker
meets the Spice Girls**

10 **Nomination**
   Illustration & Photography
   Illustration

   National Award Silver
   Title The great novels of Graham
   Greene
   Studio Geoff Grandfield
   Client The Folio Society
   Illustrator Geoff Grandfield
   Design Director Joe Whitlock-Blundell

11 **Nomination**
   Editorial

   National Award Silver
   Title Spice Girls
   Design Studio Guardian Media Group
   Client The Guardian Newspaper
   Design Director Mark Porter
   Photographer Nigel Shapran

Joe Kerr MSc (Lond)   Architectural Historian

73 Corinne Road London N19 5HA T/F 0171 609 1919

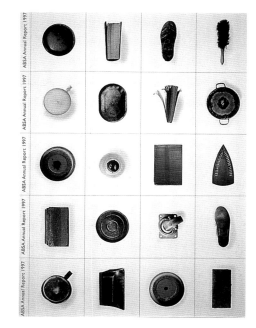

12 Graphic Design
Corporate Identity

National Award Silver
Title Joe Kerr business card
Design Studio Studio Myerscough
Client Joe Kerr
Designer Morag Myerscough

13 Graphic Design

National Award Silver
Title ABSA annual report
Design Studio Kate Stephens
Client Association For Business
Sponsorship of The Arts
Designer Kate Stephens
Photographer Mike Parsons

14 Packaging

National Award Silver
Title Pack of three handkerchiefs
Design Studio Four IV
Client National Portrait Gallery
Design Director Andy Bone
Designers Kim Hartley Jane Stanton

15 Packaging

National Award Silver
Title Joseph Parfum De Jour
Design Studio Teresa Roviras
Client Joseph
Design Director Teresa Roviras
Photographer Michael Roberts

The SL shoot had to be inte

▶ "Dear Client, unfortunately we are behind schedule with the SL shoot. As is so often the case with car shoots, the weather has got the better of us. Stuck in the studio with the sun beating down outside, our art director suddenly took off in the SL, taking the photographer with him. He was last seen on the road out of town, with the wind in his hair and a big grin on his face. No rain is forecast, so given the unfavourable conditions, it looks like we'll be unable to complete the shoot for some time.

rrupted due to the weather.

To avoid such problems in future, we should consider weather insurance for studio shoots too, especially those involving convertibles. Or next time round, we shoot somewhere where the weather isn't going to be an issue, like Iceland.

▶ Apologies for the unexpected delay and we'll keep in touch. Best regards, Springer & Jacoby."

Mercedes-Benz

FLYING
INTERNATIONAL FILM PRODUCTION COMPANY

Agency:
BGS DMB&B
Client:
BAARS
Director:
MASSIMO MAGRI'

Agency:
J.W.THOMPSON
Client:
BNL
Director:
MASSIMO MAGRI'

Agency:
DENTSU,Tokyo
Client:
DOMANI
Director:
PIETRO FOLLINI

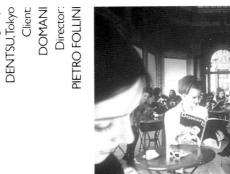
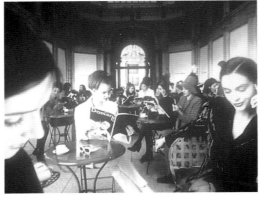

Agency:
PIRELLA GOETTSCHE LOWE
Client:
NOVA SURGELATI
Director:
ENRICO SANNIA

Agency:
LEO BURNETT
Client:
HEINEKEN
Director:
LUCA LUCINI

Agency:
BUCHOLZ&WÖRDERMANN
Bad Hömburg
Client:
SIEMENS
Director:
MAURIZIO AZZALI

Agency:
E/B/D,Dusseldorf
Client:
RAMAZZOTTI
Director:
LUIGI MONTAINI

Agency:
MILANO&GREY
Client:
MONTE DEI PASCHI di SIENA
Director:
LUIGI MONTAINI

Flying Film Production offers three
types of film production services:
Full service with the client's director;
Access to Flying's rostrum of directors
for a selection tailored to the needs of
the given script;
Complete-in-house production.

Flying Film Production
11, via Marsala
20121 Milan, Italy
Telephone: +39 02 655 2200
Telefax: +39 02 655 4783
http://www.wolf.it/flying/
e-mail: montaini@flyingfilm.it

Some of the sophisticated equipment which makes our 747's quieter.

Our aircraft have always been built to reduce engine noise. But occasionally we do detect the odd whine emanating from inside the cabin. So, for junior passengers and budding art directors, British Airways have free Skyflyers packs. Each one contains an assortment of crayons that'll keep them happily occupied during the flight. What a sound idea. **The world's favourite airline.**

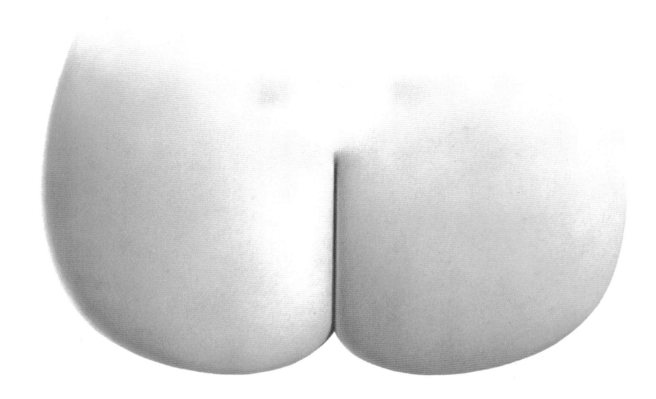

**Whether you are mentioned
in this book or not,
to us all humans are equal.**

Hakle. For absolute cleanliness.

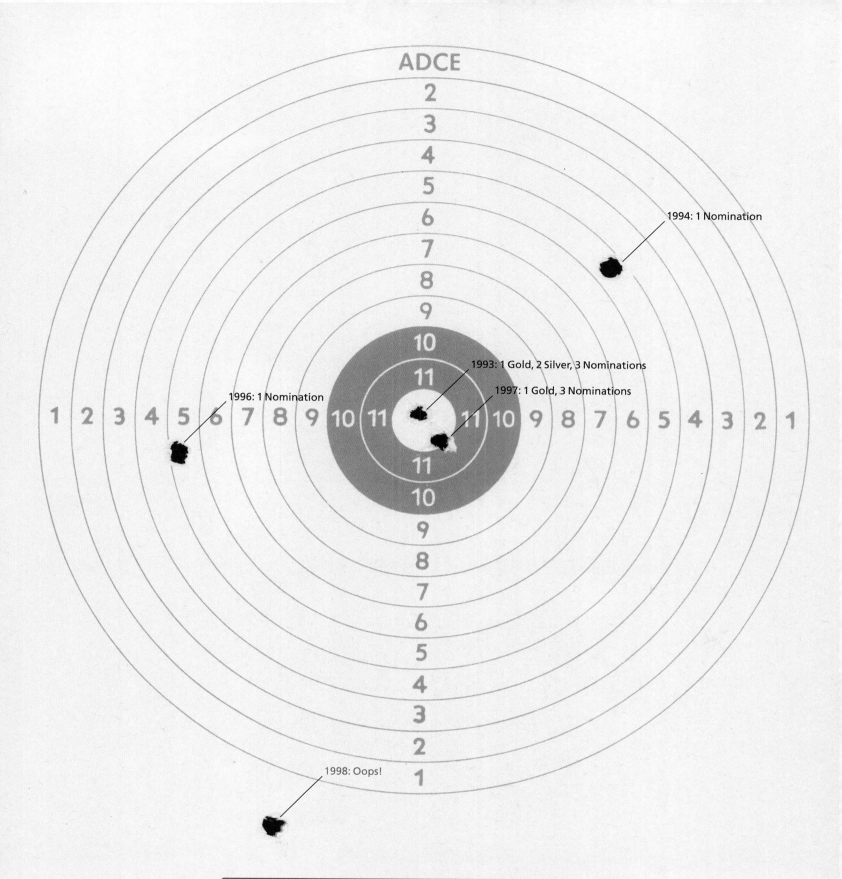

1994: 1 Nomination

1993: 1 Gold, 2 Silver, 3 Nominations

1997: 1 Gold, 3 Nominations

1996: 1 Nomination

1998: Oops!

ADCE

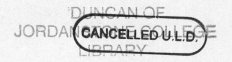

Next year we'll try again.

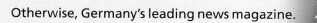

Otherwise, Germany's leading news magazine.

M. Lumpert
swissair [?]

the refreshing airline